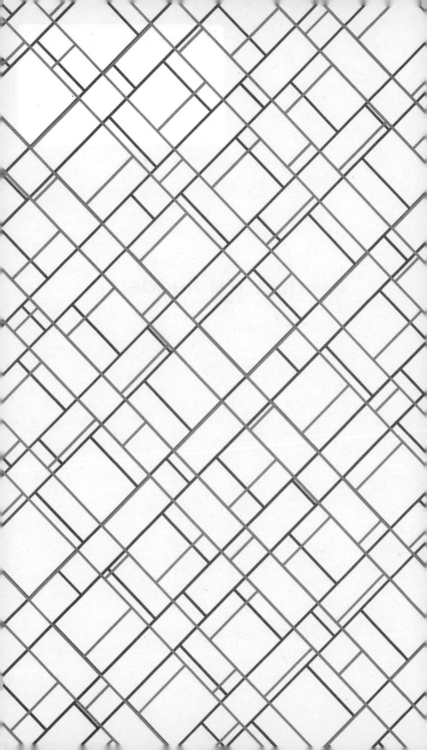

Penguin Readers

ARTIFICIAL INTELLIGENCE

BASED ON
THE ROAD TO CONSCIOUS MACHINES

BY MICHAEL WOOLDRIDGE

LEVEL

7

RETOLD BY CATRIN MORRIS
ILLUSTRATED BY MICHAEL WOOLDRIDGE
SERIES EDITOR: SORREL PITTS

This book includes content that may be distressing to readers,
including abusive or discriminatory treatment of individuals,
groups, religions or communities.

Many of the quotes in this book have been simplified
for learners of English as a foreign language.

PENGUIN BOOKS

UK | USA | Canada | Ireland | Australia
India | New Zealand | South Africa

Penguin Books is part of the Penguin Random House group of companies
whose addresses can be found at global.penguinrandomhouse.com.
www.penguin.co.uk www.puffin.co.uk www.ladybird.co.uk

Penguin
Random House
UK

The Road to Conscious Machines: The Story of AI first published by Pelican Books, 2020
This Penguin Readers edition published by Penguin Books Ltd, 2022
001

Original text written by Michael Wooldridge
Text for Penguin Readers edition adapted by Catrin Morris
Original copyright © Michael Wooldridge 2020
Text copyright © Penguin Books Ltd, 2022
Illustrated by Michael Wooldridge
Illustrations copyright © Penguin Books Ltd, 2020
Cover image copyright © buffaloboy/Shutterstock

The moral right of the original author and the original illustrator has been asserted

Printed and bound in Great Britain by Clays Ltd, Elcograf S.p.A.

The authorized representative in the EEA is Penguin Random House Ireland,
Morrison Chambers, 32 Nassau Street, Dublin D02 YH68.

A CIP catalogue record for this book is available from the British Library

ISBN: 978-0-241-54260-6

All correspondence to:
Penguin Books
Penguin Random House Children's
One Embassy Gardens, 8 Viaduct Gardens,
London SW11 7BW

MIX
Paper from
responsible sources
FSC® C018179

Penguin Random House is committed to a
sustainable future for our business, our readers
and our planet. This book is made from Forest
Stewardship Council® certified paper.

Contents

Note about the book

Michael Wooldridge, the author of this book, fell in love with **artificial intelligence** (**AI***) as a student in the 1980s and has been an AI researcher ever since. Today, he is a professor and Head of Department of Computer Science at the University of Oxford.

He was attracted to AI because it asks what it means to be human, and whether human intelligence is so special that it is impossible to recreate. He also loved the fact that AI touches on many different subjects, including: philosophy, psychology, **logic**, mathematics, economics and **robotics**.

Wooldridge has described this book as "the story of AI through failed ideas". It aims to explain what AI is and is not, and follows the journey of AI through its many high points and low points. It examines important AI developments in the past, present and future, such as: **automated translation**, driverless cars, **applications** in healthcare and wearable technology. It explores why the dream of building machines that are **self-aware**, **conscious** and **autonomous** – the image of AI that we see in books, films and on TV – is so hard to achieve. And it asks if we will ever really understand how to do this, and if we really want to.

*Definitions of words in **bold** can be found in the glossaries on pages 124–136.

Before-reading questions

1 What is artificial intelligence (AI) and how is it shown on TV, in films, books and in the media?

2 Where can you find examples of AI in your everyday life?

3 Where do you think you will find AI in the future?

4 How do you think AI could change our lives in the following areas?
   a education
   b health
   c news and information
   d safety
   e travel
   f war

CHAPTER ONE

Alan Turing and the birth of AI

You could identify many different points in history as the birth of **artificial intelligence** (**AI**), but this particular story begins at the same time as computing itself. It was in 1935, in King's College, University of Cambridge, with a brilliant young student called Alan Turing.

Today, he is about as famous as any mathematician could ever hope to be. But until the 1980s hardly anybody had heard of Alan Turing, or that he died aged just forty-one. It seems that he killed himself after he was forced to take medicine to "treat" **homosexuality**, which was then a crime. Even mathematicians and computer scientists would only have known about some of his work, as much of it was done in secret for the UK government during the Second World War, and was only made public in the 1970s.[1]

Nowadays, we all know a little about Turing thanks in part to a (very inaccurate) 2014 film called *The Imitation Game*, which tells the story of his important code-breaking work at Bletchley Park during the Second World War. But for experts researching AI and computer science, he is respected for first inventing the computer, and not long after that, for inventing the field of AI itself. Turing was extraordinary in many ways, but one of the most amazing things about him was that he invented computers by accident. As a mathematics student at the University of Cambridge in the 1930s, Turing decided to try to answer one of the main mathematical problems of the day called the *Entscheidungsproblem*, a German word for a **decision problem**. These are mathematical questions that have a yes/no answer. In 1928, mathematician David Hilbert first asked if there are decision problems that cannot be answered by simply following a **recipe** of **precise** mathematical steps. So, can these problems be reduced to simply following recipes, or computer programs, without the need for real intelligence?

When Turing took on this challenge in 1935, he not only found a solution, but he did so very quickly. Turing realized that he needed to be able to make an exact plan of a recipe that can be followed **precisely**. To do this, he invented a mathematical problem-solving machine, although it was not actually a machine, but a mathematical idea. We call these Turing machines in his honour.

A Turing machine follows the recipe it was designed for, and you can write the code for any mathematical recipe because it is so **powerful**. If all mathematical decision problems can be solved by following a recipe, then for any decision problem, you should be able to design a Turing machine to solve it. So, to return to David Hilbert's question, all you have to do is to show that there are some decision problems that cannot be answered by any Turing machine; and that is what Turing did.

Next, Turing showed that his machines could be turned

into general-purpose problem-solving machines. He designed a Turing machine that would follow any recipe that you gave it. We now call these general-purpose Turing machines Universal Turing Machines. When a computer is reduced to its simplest form, it is just that: a Universal Turing Machine made real. The programs that a computer runs are just recipes.

The way in which Turing solved the *Entscheidungsproblem* using his new invention was not only very clever, but it also helped scientists to understand if AI would be possible one day. Turing's idea was that the machines could be programmed to answer questions about other Turing machines. He considered this decision problem: if you have a Turing machine with the right information put into it, will it stop and give you an answer in the end, or could it carry on working forever?

Turing realized that there could be no recipe for checking whether a Turing machine stops, so the question "Does a Turing machine stop?" is an **undecidable problem**. In this way Turing established that there are decision problems that cannot be solved by simply following a recipe, answering Hilbert's *Entscheidungsproblem*: mathematics cannot be reduced to following recipes. With this result, Turing not only achieved one of the greatest things in twentieth-century mathematics, but he also started us on the path towards computers.

Turing did not invent his machines with the idea of actually building them, but it was not long before he and others thought about doing just that. In Munich, Germany, during the Second World War, Konrad Zuse designed a computer called the Z3 for the German government. It was not quite a modern computer, but had many of the key **ingredients** of one. Meanwhile in Pennsylvania in the United States of America, a team led by John Mauchly and J. Presper Eckert developed a machine called ENIAC to calculate information required for firing guns over long distances. And thanks to some changes made by John von Neumann, a brilliant Hungarian mathematician, ENIAC established the basic design for the modern computer, named the Von Neumann architecture in his honour.

After the Second World War, Fred Williams and Tom Kilburn built the Manchester Baby in England. This led directly to the Ferranti Mark 1, the first computer in the world that you could buy. Turing himself joined the team at Manchester University in 1948, and wrote some of the programs to run on it. By the 1950s, all the key ingredients of the modern computer had been developed, and there really were machines that could do what Turing had imagined with his mathematical idea. All you needed was enough money to buy one, and a building big enough to keep it in. These early computers were very big and used the same amount of electricity as you need for three modern homes. They have been getting smaller and cheaper ever since.

Although AI did not yet have a name, a lot of people were discussing the idea in the 1950s, and Alan Turing was one of them. He wanted to stop people saying that "machines cannot think". To do this he suggested a test, which we now call the Turing test. The basic idea for this test was the Imitation Game, a Victorian game in which someone tried to tell if another person was a man or a woman from their answers to questions. Turing thought that you could use a similar test for AI.

The way the Turing test usually works is with a human interviewer typing questions and then deciding whether a person or a computer program is answering. Turing argued that if, after enough time had passed, the interviewer still could not be certain if it were a computer program or a person, then you should accept that if it were a program then it had some sort of human-**level** intelligence. The test is brilliant because Turing avoided all the questions about whether a program was "really" intelligent, or "really" thinking, by proving that it is doing something that makes it seem exactly the same as the "real thing". However, it is important to see only the interviewer's questions and the answers rather than what is happening inside the machine; which we are not allowed to examine. Turing described his test from the point of view of a modern **digital** computer, making this the first scientific paper on AI.[2]

Although the Turing test is simple, elegant and easy to understand, it has not always been put to the best use. Programmers have often tried to trick interviewers into believing that they are dealing with a real person, rather than trying to deal with the actual issues of intelligent behaviour. The most famous example of this was a program called ELIZA, written by the German-American MIT (Massachusetts Institute of Technology) computer scientist Joseph Weizenbaum in the middle of the 1960s. ELIZA, which Weizenbaum never meant to be used in a Turing test, takes the part of a doctor asking open questions to a patient about their feelings. The program starts well, but after even a couple of sentences the conversation becomes meaningless, as ELIZA obviously does not understand what the person is saying.

It is not clear whether Turing imagined that anyone would ever actually try out his test for real, but every year programmers attempt to win $100,000 doing just that in the Loebner Prize Competition. Some critics feel that there is little point to this competition, as the programmers use tricks rather than trying to win by having a meaningful conversation that shows human-level, practical understanding. Today we also have internet chatbots, programs that attempt to talk to **users**, usually on social media and often using little more than conversations built on keywords, just like ELIZA did. Chatbots of this kind are not AI.

CHAPTER TWO
What is AI and what can it do?

After the Second World War, newspapers across the world announced that scientists had invented "electronic brain" machines which could do lots of highly **complex** mathematics, more quickly and more accurately than humans could. They must have seemed like very intelligent machines. In fact, these electronic brains were doing something incredibly useful, and something that people find very difficult to do, but not something that requires intelligence. Understanding exactly what computers are designed to do, and what they cannot do, is central to understanding AI, and why it is so difficult.

Remember that Turing machines and computers are nothing more than machines for following instructions. The instructions that we give a Turing machine are what we call a program nowadays. Most programmers probably do not even realize that they are basically **interacting** with a Turing machine. We build higher-level programming languages like Python, Java and C, which make it easier to use the machine, by hiding some of the confusing information about it from the programmer. However, programming with these languages is still complex, which is why good programmers are so well paid.

Without explaining how to program a computer, it is enough to know that every program basically follows instructions like:

- Add A to B;
- If the result is bigger than C, then do D, if not, do E;
- Repeatedly do F until G.

This is true for computer programs like Microsoft Word and PowerPoint, games like *Call of Duty* and *Minecraft*, social media, the **apps** on your phone, or internet search engines. If we are going to build intelligent machines, then it must be possible to reduce their intelligence to such simple, precise instructions. This is the basic challenge of AI. To make it possible, we must create machines that behave intelligently, by following lists of simple instructions like these.

To begin to understand what computers can do well, we need to realize just how fast they are. The kind of computer you might own today can follow up to 100 billion instructions (like those listed above) every second. To do the same number of calculations that a computer can do in just one second, you would have to follow one instruction every ten seconds without stopping for 3,700 years.

As well as being much slower than computers, humans make more mistakes. Although computers often crash, this is usually because of mistakes made by the people who wrote the programs. Modern computers rarely make mistakes. They can be trusted to work for up to 50,000 hours, following tens of billions of instructions for every second of those hours, before failing.

Finally, despite being just machines for following instructions, this does not mean that computers cannot make decisions.

They certainly can, but we have to give them precise instructions about how. And a computer can later change these instructions for itself, as long as we have told it how to do so. A computer is able to behave differently over time – it can learn.

So, if computers can follow very simple instructions very, very quickly, and they can make decisions, as long as those decisions are precisely explained, why is advanced AI hard to achieve? To understand this, it helps to look at problems which are easy to write the code for and problems which are not.

Mathematical calculations are the easiest for computers because they can be done following very simple recipes which can be directly **translated** into computer programs. (The first program Turing wrote for the Manchester Baby computer in 1948 did this.)

Next, we have **tasks** like arranging lists of numbers, from low to high, or names from A to Z. The early recipes for this type of task were very slow and almost impossible to use. Then, in 1959, a **technique** called QuickSort was invented, which for the first time provided a really **efficient** way to do this.

Problems that required much more effort, such as playing board games, were a big challenge. Although there is a very simple recipe for playing board games **based** on a technique called **search**, which is easy to program, it only works on very simple games, as it requires a lot of time and computer memory. To make search work with more complex games, something extra was needed; there will be more about this in Chapter Four.

The next group of problems: recognizing faces in a picture, **automated translation** and usable real-time translation of spoken words, are all very different, but have been solved by a technique called **machine learning**, which will be discussed in Chapter Eleven.

The area of driverless cars seems simple as we do not usually think intelligence is needed to drive. In fact, it is very hard to get computers to drive cars. The main problem is that a car needs to understand where it is, and what is going on around it. Imagine a driverless car on a busy city road. The main difficulty is not deciding what to do (slow down, speed up, turn left, right, etc.), but rather identifying where it is, where the other cars and people are, and what they are doing. If you have all that information, then deciding what you need to do is usually going to be easy; but more about that in Chapter Twelve.

There are some problems that we really have little idea how to solve using AI. These include: understanding a complex story and answering questions about it; translating a novel; understanding what is happening in a photograph and not just recognising the people in it; writing an interesting story; or understanding a painting. But the most difficult problem of all is how to develop computers with general-purpose human-level intelligence. The Turing test, as discussed in the previous chapter, raises many questions about this.

Imagine that you are an interviewer in the Turing test and you believe that you are talking to something that understands your questions and produces the kinds of answers that a human might give. According to the Turing test, the program is behaving like a human and that makes the decision that you are interacting with something with human-level intelligence simple. But there are still at least two different **logical** ways of explaining this: either the program actually understands the conversation, like a person does; or the program does not understand the conversation, but it seems to understand. There is a big difference between these two positions. Most of us would probably accept that the second type of program is possible, but that the first is more difficult to imagine, and we would need more evidence. The goal of building programs that really do understand in the way that people understand is called **strong AI**; the weaker goal, of building programs that show the same ability as humans, but without really understanding, is called **weak AI**.

While the grand dream of AI seems obvious, it is surprisingly hard to identify what it means, or when we will know that we have found it. For this reason, although strong AI is important, it has little to do with AI research today. A more limited goal is to build machines that have general-purpose human-level intelligence, known as **General AI**. This would mean a computer that has all the same intelligence abilities as a **typical** person, able to: talk in natural language, solve problems, use **logic**, understand its environment, and so on. It probably would not involve issues such as **consciousness**. So General AI might be thought of as weak AI. Instead, what AI researchers usually concentrate on is building computer programs that can carry out particular tasks which normally require our brains to do them. But how?

Historically, AI has followed one of two main ways of approaching this problem. The first, called **symbolic AI**, involves trying to **model** how the human mind works in everyday tasks like **problem solving**. For example, a **symbol** "room451" in a robot's control **system** might be the name that a robot uses for your bedroom, and a symbol "cleanRoom" might be used as the name for the activity of cleaning a room. As the robot works out what to do, it makes use of these symbols, and so, for example, if the robot decides to carry out the action "cleanRoom(room451)", then this means that the robot has decided to clean your bedroom. The symbols the robot is using mean something in its environment. This was the most popular way of building AI systems until the end of the 1980s, maybe because it was clear and it modelled the way humans think.

The second way of building an AI system is to try to model the human brain, but this is extremely complex. A human brain contains about 100 billion parts which are connected to each other, and we really do not, and probably never will, understand how they work well enough to copy them into a machine. But we can look at how the brain works and try to make a **model** of its different parts in intelligent systems. This research area is called neural **networks**, or **neural nets**. First developed before the birth of AI itself, it has shown most progress this century and led to a new interest in AI.

CHAPTER THREE
The Golden Age of AI

By the end of the 1950s, a new field of study had been established and the Golden Age of AI had begun. There were many AI systems built in this period, like SHRDLU, STRIPS and SHAKEY. Compared to modern computers, the machines used to build these systems were incredibly limited, slow and hard to use. The tools that we depend on now for developing programs were not available then, and even if they had been, could not have run on these computers. AI researchers often had to work at night because these computers were used for more important work during the day. They also had to invent all sorts of clever programming tricks to make the programs work at all.

In the summer of 1956, the field of AI was given its name by a brilliant, young American academic called John McCarthy. During the 1950s and 1960s, McCarthy developed a range of ideas in computing that we cannot imagine not knowing about today. One of the most famous things he developed was LISP, a programming language popular with AI researchers, which is still regularly taught and used across the world.

While working as a young professor at Dartmouth College in New Hampshire in 1955, McCarthy applied to the Rockefeller Institute for money to organize a summer school for international researchers with similar interests. The Dartmouth summer school brought together most of the researchers who would be key to the future development of AI. As well as academics, people from the fields of industry, government, the military and other important groups attended the summer school. The USA typically developed computer technology by having people from different fields working together, which would establish it as the international leader in AI for years to come.

When applying for the Rockefeller money, McCarthy had to give a name to the summer school and he chose "artificial intelligence". Some people later regretted this choice of name as artificial also means **fake**, which can sound negative; and many of the tasks that AI researchers work on do not require any intelligence to do them. Despite this, and an absence of any real progress in AI by the end of the summer school, a new academic field with McCarthy's chosen name was here to stay.

The period following the Dartmouth summer school was one of exciting developments and fast progress for AI. Four people who attended would go on to be among the most important researchers in AI. McCarthy himself started an AI laboratory at Stanford University, in the heart of what is now Silicon Valley. Marvin Minsky started the AI lab at MIT. Alan Newell and Herb Simon went to Carnegie Mellon University.

But by the middle of the 1970s, the good times were over for AI. As we have seen, General AI is a large and imprecise goal, which cannot easily be approached directly. During the Golden

Age, instead of starting to build a complete general intelligent system, researchers tried to identify the various **capabilities** that seemed to be required for general-purpose AI, and to build systems to show these different capabilities. The idea was that if these systems could be built, it would be possible to put them all together later.

The first of these capabilities was **perception**, which seemed simple, but is in fact extremely difficult to achieve. A machine that is going to act intelligently needs to be able to get information about its environment. Human perception of the world comes from sight, sound, touch, smell and taste. As a result, one of the AI research areas involved building perception **sensors**. Robots today use a wide range of artificial sensors to give them information about their environment, but building these complex sensors is only part of the problem. However good a digital camera is, it simply breaks down the image it is seeing into squares and gives each one a number to show colour and brightness. So, a robot with the best digital camera will, in the end, only receive a long list of numbers. The challenge is to read those numbers and understand what it is seeing. This has so far proved to be more difficult than actually building the sensors.

Another key capability for general intelligent systems seems to be the ability to learn from experience, also called machine learning. This is not like human learning; it is about learning from and making **predictions** based on **data**. For example, machine learning has had recent success in programs that can recognize faces in pictures. This is done by providing lots of pictures with labels next to the people that appear in them. The program should then learn to correctly identify a person in a picture without the label.

Problem solving and **planning** are two capabilities that can be linked to each other and to programs behaving intelligently. Both capabilities require a precise series of actions to achieve a goal; the challenge is to arrange these actions correctly. Playing a board game such as **chess** is an example of this. The goal is to win the game; the actions are all the possible ways to move; the challenge is to work out which move to choose. One of the biggest difficulties in problem solving and planning is that, while the programming idea might be easy, when you come to write the steps there are just too many possibilities.

Reasoning or using logic is perhaps the highest capability linked to intelligence, as it involves gaining new knowledge from facts already known. Automated reasoning is all about giving computers the capability to **reason logically**. This idea has long been an important part of AI, as we will see in Chapter Six, but it is no longer its main goal.

Finally, there is natural language understanding, or programs that can interact in ordinary, natural human languages like English and Chinese. Programs are at present coded using an artificial language such as Python, Java or C, but these are much simpler than natural human languages. So while it is possible to produce precise rules for computer languages, it has proved impossible to do this with natural languages, which are used in everyday situations, and change too easily to fit such rules.

———————

SHRDLU was one of the great AI systems of the Golden Age. Its strange name comes from the way letters were arranged on printing machines of the time. Developed by Stanford University student Terry Winograd in 1971, SHRDLU aimed to show two key capabilities: problem solving and natural language understanding. The problem-solving part of SHRDLU was based on one of AI's most famous experimental **scenarios**: the **Blocks World**. To make the problem easier to manage, a **simulated** environment containing a number of coloured objects was used, rather than trying to build a real robot. Problem solving in the SHRDLU Blocks World involves arranging objects using a simulated robot arm, according to instructions from a user. Its **limitation** is that you can only use a small range of actions:

- Pick up object x from the table;
- Place object x on the table;
- Pick up object x from object y;
- Place object x on top of object y.

Everything that happens in the Blocks World is reduced to these actions, but the robot is limited in what it is able to do. For example, the robot arm will only be able to pick up object x from the table if object x is on the table and the robot arm is empty.

The Blocks World is probably the most studied scenario in the whole of AI, because we can imagine robots doing such tasks in the real world. But the Blocks World as it appears in SHRDLU is extremely limited as a scenario for developing useful AI techniques. Firstly, the Blocks World is closed, so the only thing that causes change is SHRDLU itself; this would not be true in the real world. Secondly, and perhaps more importantly, the Blocks World is simulated. SHRDLU is not actually picking up objects and moving them around with a robot arm. Getting robots to move even simple objects in the real world is still a very difficult challenge today.

The system also uses a model of the world, modelling how its actions might affect this world. But it never actually looks at the real world to build its model, or to check that it is correct. Researchers argued that it ignored difficult problems that a robot would actually face. So, although logical and easy to explain, the Blocks World is limited by only trying to deal with a small part of the robot's problems.

However, one of the things people most liked about SHRDLU was that not only could the user give instructions and receive answers in ordinary English, but conversations were richer and more natural than with a system like ELIZA. But it became clear that SHRDLU was only able to produce rich conversations because they were linked to the controlled scenario of the Blocks World. Despite all these limitations, SHRDLU was still an important moment in the development of AI systems.

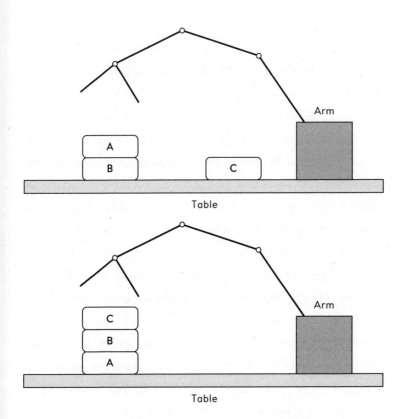

**The Blocks World: a robot arm working
in a simulated environment**

CHAPTER FOUR
Limitations and problems

As robots have often been linked to AI in the media, it is little surprise that people think of AI as robots behaving like humans. But robots actually played a small part in the AI story during the Golden Age, as they were expensive, slow and difficult to build. Programs like SHRDLU, which worked in a simulated world, were easier and much cheaper to build than robots that worked in the real world. However, there was one amazing experiment with AI robots at the Stanford Research Institute (SRI) between 1966 and 1972: the SHAKEY project.

SHAKEY was the first serious attempt to build a **mobile** robot that could be given tasks in the real world, and work out how to perform them on its own. It could **perceive** its environment, understand where it was and what was around it. It could receive tasks from users, plan and perform them, while making sure it was achieving the project's aims.

———

As with SHRDLU, the tasks involved moving objects such as boxes around an office environment, but SHAKEY was a real robot, moving real objects – a much bigger challenge. SHAKEY needed to combine a lot of different AI capabilities to succeed. The developers had to build a robot small enough to move quickly and easily around an office, with powerful and accurate sensors for the robot to understand its environment. For this, SHAKEY had a television camera and range-finders, special technology for working out its distance from objects. It also had technology to help it perceive things in its way. To **navigate** around the office and plan how to do the tasks it was given, developers designed a system called STRIPS (Stanford Research Institute Problem Solver), which is now generally recognized as one of the earliest AI planning techniques. All these capabilities had to work well together, and as any AI researcher will tell you, getting one of these capabilities to work is a challenge, but getting them all to work at the same time is even harder.

————

However, as clever as it was, SHAKEY's capabilities also showed the limitations of the AI technology of the time. To make SHAKEY work, its designers had to limit the challenges the robot faced. For example, SHAKEY could only perceive **obstacles** with the help of a specially painted and lit environment. And because the TV camera required so much **power**, it was only switched on when it was needed, and took about ten seconds to produce an image. The limitations of computers at that time were also a problem for the developers. In the fifteen minutes it took SHAKEY to work out how to do a task, it would do nothing while it sent a message by radio to a computer which was powerful enough to run the program, but too big and heavy for the robot to carry around. SHAKEY could not possibly have been used on any practical problem, but it was maybe the first

autonomous mobile robot and helped develop many new AI technologies.

––––––––––

The ability to solve problems is one of the key capabilities that makes humans different from other animals. If we can build programs that can solve problems that people find hard, then surely this would be an important step on the road to AI. For this reason, problem solving was carefully studied in the Golden Age. Computers were often required to solve the kind of problems you find on the **puzzle** page of a newspaper, as an AI test. The Towers of Hanoi is a typical example of such a puzzle.

In the Towers of Hanoi there are three posts and sixty-four golden rings. The rings are of different sizes and can lie over the posts. At the beginning all the rings are on the furthest left post, and are then moved one by one between the posts; the aim being to move all the rings to the furthest right post, but following two rules:

1. Only one ring can be moved at a time between the posts;

2. At no time can any ring lie on a smaller ring.

So how do you move all the rings from left to right, without breaking these rules? It can be done by using a technique called search, a basic AI problem-solving technique, which involves **systematically** considering all possible plans of action. Any program that plays a game like chess will be based on search, as will the **satellite navigation system** in your car. It is one of the basic techniques in AI. As in the Blocks World, we want to find a **sequence** of actions that will take us from an **initial state** to our **goal state**. We can use search to solve problems like the Towers of Hanoi as follows:

- First, starting from the initial state, we consider the effects of every available action on that initial state. The effect of performing an action **transforms** the problem into a new state.

- If one of the actions has led to the goal state, then we have succeeded: the solution to the puzzle is the sequence of actions that got us from the initial state to the goal state.

- If not, we repeat this **process** for every state we achieved, considering the effect of each action on those states, and so on.

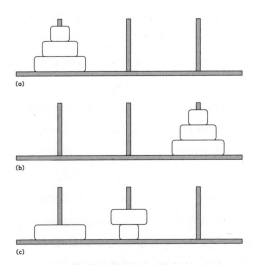

The Towers of Hanoi,
the type of puzzle studied in the Golden Age of AI

Applying this recipe for search generates a **search tree**. So, in the Towers of Hanoi:

- First, we can only move the smallest ring, and our only choices are to move it to the middle or furthest right post. We have two possible actions available, and two possible states.

- If we choose to move the small ring to the centre post, that then gives us three possible available actions: we can move the smallest ring to the furthest left post or the furthest right post, or we can move the middle-sized ring to the furthest right post (not to the centre post, because then it would be on top of the smallest ring, which is against the rules) . . . and so on.

Because we are systematically generating the search tree, level by level, we are considering all possibilities – and so, if there is a solution, we will definitely find it in the end using this process. It is called an exhaustive search, because it investigates every possible move at every step. It is quite easy to write a program for this kind of exhaustive search, which would make the task much easier for a computer than for a person. To solve the Towers of Hanoi problem, working with three rings, the smallest number of times you would need to move is seven. If you did a quick experiment, you would see that in almost all possible combinations of the puzzle there would be three ways to move, so the **branching factor** is three. However, different search problems will have different branching factors, and these can create search trees too big for the memory of an average computer. Even if their technology improved, they would not be able to deal with search trees this large. This is true of a board game called Go, which quickly reaches up to 3.9 billion states in its search tree only a little way into the game. After that the numbers get much higher!

The problem of search trees growing at such a crazy speed is called **combinatorial explosion**, and it is the most important practical problem in AI. You would need to find a sure recipe for solving search problems quickly. And you would need to achieve the same result as an exhaustive search, but without all that effort. If you could do all of that, you would become very famous and many problems that are now very difficult for AI would suddenly be easy. But it is impossible to get around combinatorial explosion: you have to work with it.

CHAPTER FIVE

Combinatorial explosion

Combinatorial explosion has long been recognized as a central problem of AI. It was one of the topics studied at McCarthy's 1956 summer school. Attention very quickly moved to making search more efficient, for example by building the tree along just one branch, rather than developing it level by level. This is called **depth-first search**, and it allows you to expand a branch until you either get a solution, or are certain that you will not. If you are ever unable to move forward, you stop expanding that branch, and go back up the tree to work on the next branch. The best thing about depth-first search is that you do not have to save the whole of the search tree on your system, only the branch you are working on. The worst thing about it is that if you explore the wrong branch, you may go on expanding your search without ever finding a solution. You really need to know which branch to investigate.

This is what **heuristic search** tries to do, using experience rather than **theory** to decide where to search. In most cases we cannot find **heuristics** that will send our search in the best possible direction. But we can often find heuristics for the particular problems we are interested in solving, although they will not always perform well.

Heuristic search is such a natural idea that it has been

reinvented many times over the years, but it was first applied to an AI program in the mid-1950s. Arthur Samuel, who worked for the company IBM, used it to write a program to play the game of **checkers**.

Samuel's idea established the use of board games to test AI techniques, which is still done today. It was based on heuristic search; and was the first real machine learning program, teaching itself to play. The program could play quite a good game of checkers, which is incredible considering the basic computers of the time. Most importantly, it estimated how "good" any position on the board was for a particular player. By combining information to give the quality of a board position, it worked out how likely a player was to win. For example, the more pieces you have on the board, the better you are playing. A typical heuristic would then involve moving to the best board position. But in practice this is not enough to win at checkers, a game played against another player whose actions you have to consider. Samuel's program guessed that the other player would always move in the worst possible way for you. This "worst case reasoning" approach is called minimax search, and is an important idea in game playing. It involves acting to get the highest score for yourself, while imagining that the other player acts to get you the lowest possible score.

This approach to heuristic search was greatly improved at the end of the 1960s, with the work of Nils Nilsson's team at SRI. They developed a technique called A* as part of the

SHAKEY project, which identified some simple rules that allow us to know when a heuristic is "good". Before A*, heuristic search was nothing more than a guessing game; after A*, it was a well-understood mathematical process. Now considered one of the basic **algorithms** in computing, A* is widely used today for satellite navigation systems in cars. But A* only leads to a solution if it uses the right heuristic, and gives us no answer to the problem of how to find good heuristics for particular problems.

By the 1960s, it was clear that whether a problem is undecidable or not was far from being the end of the story. The fact that a problem was **decidable**, according to Turing's work, did not mean that it could be solved at all in any practical way, as it might require impossible amounts of memory, or simply take too long. It was becoming obvious that many AI problems fell into this group. Here is an example of a problem that shows just this point:

You have four people working for you in your office: John, Paul, George and Ringo. You need a team of three people for a particular project. Because of their characters, John and Paul cannot work together.

Can you find a good team? In this case there are two solutions: either John, George and Ringo, or Paul, George and Ringo. Now suppose we add a further obstacle: John and George cannot work together. Can we still find a team? Yes: Paul, George and Ringo. Now if we add one final obstacle – Paul and George cannot work together – the answer to our problem becomes "no": there is no team of three people that can work together.

The problem we are considering is: a list of n people (in the example they are John, Paul, George and Ringo, so $n = 4$), and a list of "impossible pairs" (for example John and Paul who cannot work together). We are given a number, m, and we are asked whether it is possible to find a team of exactly m people from the list, avoiding the impossible pairs. It seems easy to see the answer to this problem, and it is a simple recipe to program on a computer. But look at what happens when the numbers get bigger.

If you have ten workers and you want a team of five, you have 252 possibilities to look at. The problem is boring but not difficult. Now suppose you have 100 people, and you need a team of fifty. Then you would have to check 100 billion billion billion possible teams. A fast modern computer might be able to evaluate 10 billion possible teams every second – which sounds a lot, until you realize that it would still need far, far more time to investigate all the alternatives than is available before the end of the universe! At present, we cannot improve computer technology enough to check all these possibilities in a sensible amount of time. This is another example of combinatorial explosion, like we saw when looking at search trees. So, although our basic approach of systematically searching through all the possible teams works in theory, it is not going to be practical.

As we noted earlier, simple exhaustive search is a very basic technique. You could use heuristics, or another technique that could improve your chances a bit, but in the end you will not be able to avoid the combinatorial explosion. Any recipe you find that is sure to solve this problem is not going to be practical for most cases. This is called an **NP-complete problem**: a problem for which it is hard to find solutions (because there are too many of them to check with an exhaustive search), but where it is easy to check whether you have found a solution (in our team-building example, we can check a possible solution by simply making sure that it does not have any impossible pairs).

There is one other important thing about NP-complete problems. To understand it, we need to introduce the travelling salesman problem. A man on a business trip must visit a number of cities, returning finally to his starting point. He can drive for a certain distance with his car full of petrol. Is there a way to visit all the cities and return to the starting point, with the amount of petrol in his car? The problem appears similar to our team-building scenario; we can solve it by listing all the possible ways between the cities, and checking whether we have enough petrol. However, as you can probably guess, the number of possible ways increases quickly as the number of cities increases. For ten cities, you would have to consider up to 3.6 million possible ways; for eleven cities, up to 40 million. So, the travelling salesman problem suffers from the same combinatorial explosion as the team-building problem. They might appear to be completely different, but in fact NP-complete problems can all easily be transformed into each other.

Imagine there were a recipe that was sure to quickly give the correct answer to any team-building problem. You could then take the travelling salesman problem and quickly transform it into a team-building problem, which the recipe would quickly solve. This means that if you could find a quick recipe, or program, for solving just one NP-complete problem, then you would have found a recipe for solving all of them.

So far nobody has found an efficient recipe for any NP-complete problem. And the question of whether they can be **efficiently** solved is one of the most important open problems in science today. It is known as the P vs NP problem and you can find it everywhere: in problem solving, game playing, planning, learning and reasoning.

By the end of the 1970s the difficulty in solving these problems had led to a loss of confidence in AI, which translated into a reduction in the money available to research it. This period became known as the AI winter.

CHAPTER SIX

New hope and interest

For the next ten years, new researchers developed knowledge-based **expert systems** rather than working on General AI. These could solve precise, but limited problems, which humans take many years to learn how to solve, so there are few experts. Industry also started putting a lot of money into AI, as it could see for the first time how to make money out of it.

Knowledge-based AI was based on an important new idea: that human knowledge about a problem should be **explicitly** captured and used within an AI system. The usual way of doing this was based on rules. A rule in AI captures a precise piece of knowledge and presents it as "if . . . then . . ." For example[3]:

- IF animal can fly AND animal lays eggs THEN animal is bird.

Each rule has an antecedent (the part after the "IF") and a **consequent** (the part after the "THEN"). So, in the example above, the antecedent is "animal can fly AND animal lays eggs", while the consequent is "animal is bird". If the information we have correctly matches the antecedent, then the rule works and we can reason that the consequent is true. This **conclusion** gives us more information, which can then be used in later rules to get more information, and so on. Expert systems generally interacted with a human user who was responsible for providing information to the system and answering questions asked by the system.

One of the earliest expert systems in the 1970s was called MYCIN, developed at Stanford University to help doctors give expert advice about blood diseases in humans. MYCIN showed for the first time that AI systems could solve important problems better than human experts. Many later systems were based on it. The project was successful because real experts worked with the expert system; projects often failed when this was not the case. Over about five years MYCIN's knowledge was written in code and improved until it contained hundreds of rules.

MYCIN was important because it had all the key qualities of expert systems. First, the system interacted as humans do with questions and answers, which has become the typical model for expert systems. And MYCIN's main job was **diagnosis**, which has become the typical task for expert systems. Second, MYCIN could explain its reasoning, which became very important for **applications** of AI. If an AI system like MYCIN is working on a problem which can result in life or death, it is important that people are confident in what it advises them to do. Finally, MYCIN could deal with **uncertainty**, which has since become a major topic of research in AI. In MYCIN's case it was possible that the result of a user's blood test could be incorrect. To make good decisions, expert systems need to carefully consider lots of different evidence. To do this MYCIN used a technique called certainty factors, where a number is given to the level of belief in a particular piece of information. MYCIN performed its tasks as well as experts, and better than family doctors.

DENDRAL was another exciting expert system that appeared in the 1970s. This project, also from Stanford University, was led by Ed Feigenbaum, who is often considered the "father of expert systems". DENDRAL aimed to help chemists find out the chemical make-up of things. By the middle of the 1980s, DENDRAL was being used by hundreds of people every day.

The Digital Equipment Corporation (DEC) developed the R1/XCON system to help make its VAX computers. By the end of the 1980s R1/XCON had about 17,500 rules, and it is said that it saved the company about $40 million. Just as MYCIN showed it could perform better than human experts, DENDRAL showed that expert systems could be useful, and R1/XCON showed that they could make money. Anybody comfortable with programming could be taught the basics of expert systems, and building expert systems seemed easier than building normal computer programs. The future of AI was once more bright, at least for intelligent knowledge-based systems.

Although rules became the main approach to capturing human knowledge, they were too simple to capture knowledge about complex environments. Researchers wanted to understand what the knowledge in their expert systems actually meant, and to provide a true mathematical basis for knowledge-based systems. The solution in the late 1970s was to use logic, which was developed to understand reasoning and, in particular, to separate good reasoning from bad reasoning. Let's consider an example of good reasoning:

- All humans are going to die.
- Emma is human.
- So, Emma is going to die.

Now consider the next example:

- All professors are good-looking.
- Michael is a professor.
- So, Michael is good-looking.

While we were happy to accept "All humans are going to die", we probably would not agree that "All professors are good-looking". However, from a logical point of view, the reasoning in this example is perfectly good. If all professors were good-looking, and Michael were a professor, then it would be logical to **conclude** that Michael was good-looking. Logic does not care whether the sentences you start from (the premises) are actually true. It simply depends on whether you can accept the pattern of reasoning, and the conclusions you come to, if the premises were true.

The next example, however, shows some bad reasoning:

- All students are hard-working.
- Sophie is a student.
- So, Sophie is rich.

Here the pattern of reasoning is not good because, although Sophie may be rich, it is not logical to conclude that Sophie is rich from the two premises. So, logic is all about patterns of reasoning and it tells us when we can safely come to conclusions from certain premises. This process is called **deduction**.

The system that provides the language supporting almost all work in mathematics is called **first-order logic**, and when applied to AI it is **logic-based AI**. In logic-based AI an "**agent**" (here it is the AI system) can take some "sentences in logic" like: "All humans are going to die" and "All professors are good-looking". It can then **deduce** the actions required to achieve its goals[4]. First-order logic provides a rich, mathematically precise language with which such sentences can be shown.

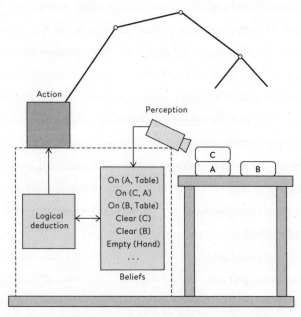

Logic-based AI as applied to the Blocks World scenario

Logic-based AI was important because it made everything simple. The problem of building an intelligent system was reduced to writing a clear, logical description of what a robot should do. To understand why a system did something, you just looked at its beliefs and its reasoning. Logic-based AI grew so popular that researchers began to think it might be usefully applied across the whole of computing. With logic programming, as it became known, you use the power of logic to say what you know about a problem without writing a recipe, as a logic program would deduce what it needed to do.

Logic programming was based on a language called PROLOG which is still used and taught across the world every day. Logic programming provides a different way of thinking about computing and computer problems and how to solve them.

The Cyc project was probably the most famous experiment in this period of knowledge-based AI, developed by Doug Lenat, who became sure that the idea of "Knowledge is power" provided the key to General AI. So, with a group of researchers Lenat began the task of creating a huge **knowledge base** for Cyc, which would need a complete description of the world as we understand it. All the everyday knowledge that an average person has would need to be written down in Cyc's own special language and put into the system. Lenat estimated the project would require 200 person years of effort, but hoped that before too long Cyc would be able to teach itself. Despite or because Cyc's aims were incredibly ambitious, the project received research money from the Microelectronics and Computer Consortium (MCC) in Austin, Texas, in 1984.

The project was started, but it did not work. The first problem was knowing where to begin and what language to use. The team quickly discovered that their original ideas about how to organize the knowledge that Cyc would use were too simple and imprecise, so they found they had to start again. But after ten years, Lenat was still full of hope and his project caught the attention of Vaughan Pratt, a computer science professor at Stanford University. When Pratt was shown what Cyc could do, it soon became obvious that Cyc could not give meaningful answers to many of more than 100 basic questions about our world. These included: Which is wetter, land or sea? Can a car drive backwards? How long can people go without air?

Cyc may not have delivered General AI, but it taught us a lot about the development and organization of large knowledge-based systems. Maybe Cyc was just ahead of its time, as thirty years after the Cyc project began, Google announced the knowledge graph to develop their search services. It is a similar large knowledge base, but one key difference is that the Google system's knowledge is **automatically** taken from web pages like Wikipedia. It is not clear how much reasoning it actually does, but you could say that Cyc lives on in Google's knowledge graph.

CHAPTER SEVEN
Behavioural AI

By the late 1980s, the progress of expert systems had slowed, and the AI world was once more accused of promising too much but delivering too little. This time people not only questioned the idea of "Knowledge is power", but also many of the basic ideas behind AI in general, and symbolic AI in particular. Australian-born **robotics** expert Rodney Brooks was one of the strongest and most unlikely critics of AI. His main interest was in building robots that could do useful tasks in the real world. In the 1980s, he became fed up with the idea that the key to building such robots was to write code with knowledge about the world that they could use to reason and make decisions. After taking up a position at MIT, he started working on his plan to rethink AI at its most basic level.

To understand Brooks' arguments, it is helpful to remember the Blocks World: a simulated environment made up of a table, with several different objects which can be moved in particular ways. At first it seems like a good test for AI techniques, as it sounds like the kind of task a robot might have to do in the real world. But for Brooks and his supporters, the Blocks World was fake, because it is simulated and ignores things that would be difficult in the real world, such as perception.

Brooks' position was based on three key points. Firstly, he

thought that meaningful progress in AI could only be achieved with systems in real-world situations, which they perceived and acted upon. Secondly, he argued that you can produce intelligent behaviour without the kind of **explicit** knowledge and reasoning of knowledge-based AI in general, and logic-based AI in particular. Finally, he believed that intelligence is an **emergent property** that comes from something interacting with its environment.

By the early 1990s AI was divided into the McCarthy, Stanford University, old-world view of logic, **knowledge representation** and reasoning; and the Brooks, MIT, new-world view of AI, which not only rejected the old-world view, but made fun of it. In the McCarthy view of logical AI, the system is separated from the environment. Suppose you have a robot designed to choose the best action to perform according to the McCarthy model of logical AI; let's consider how this works over time.

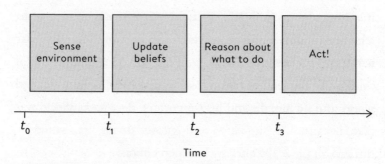

The logical AI system robot chooses the best time to act

At time t_0 through to time t_1, the robot **senses** its environment, then it takes from t_1 to t_2 to **process** this sensor data and **update** the robot's beliefs. Between t_2 and t_3 the robot reasons about what action to perform, and finally, at time t_3, the robot starts to act on its decision. If the idea was that the robot always made the best decision about what to perform, is the action that it chooses the best action at time t_1 or time t_3? The robot got the information about its environment no later than t_1, but only starts to act on this information at t_3, making this approach impractical because of the time that has passed. Surprisingly, until the late 1980s, almost all AI research was based on building machines which could make the best decision in theory (as long as the world did not change while they considered what to do), rather than the best decision in practice.

Had Brooks been just another critic of AI it is unlikely that his ideas would have gained much support, as the AI world was used to ignoring its critics and carrying on anyway. But Brooks went on to develop a different theory and to expertly show how it worked. It was known as **behavioural AI** because it called attention to particular **behaviours**, each of which played a part in the way an intelligent system worked. The technique followed by Brooks was called the **subsumption architecture**, and seems to have had the most lasting effect of any idea from that period.

Let's see how the subsumption architecture can be used to build a simple but useful **vacuum cleaner** robot like the popular

Roomba robot, which Brooks designed for his company iRobot. The robot has to travel around a building, avoiding obstacles and **vacuuming** when it perceives dirt. When the robot has a low battery, or its dirt container is full, it should return to its **docking station** and shut down.

For the basic method of the subsumption architecture, the different robot behaviours must be identified. Then the robot can be built, getting it to show one of the behaviours, then gradually adding others. The key challenge is to work out how these behaviours are linked to each other, and to organize them so that the robot shows the right behaviour at the right time. This typically requires doing a lot of experiments with the robot.

The vacuum cleaning robot requires six behaviours:

• Avoid obstacles: If I perceive an obstacle, then I change direction, choosing a new direction at **random**.

• Shut down: If I am at the docking station and have a low battery, then I shut down.

• Empty dirt: If I am at the docking station and am carrying dirt, then I empty the dirt container.

• Return to dock: If the battery is low or the dirt container is full, then I return to the docking station.

• Vacuum: If I perceive dirt at the present position then I switch on the vacuum.

• Walk **randomly**: I choose a direction at random and I move in that direction.

To organize these behaviours, Brooks suggested using a

subsumption hierarchy which decides the importance of each. Behaviours lower in the hierarchy are more important than those further up. So, for example, avoiding obstacles is a task which the robot will always do if it faces any. It is easy to see how these behaviours, organized into a hierarchy, will solve the problem: the robot will search for dirt, and vacuum when it finds dirt, as long as it is not low on power or the dirt container is full. It will return to its docking station if the battery is low or the dirt container is full.

Although the behaviours in our vacuum cleaning robot look like rules, they are in fact much simpler and do not require the same effort as logical reasoning. In fact, they can be directly applied as simple electrical **circuits**, so the robot will react to changing data very quickly and not be separated from its environment.

Brooks went on to develop and build a lot of important robots using the subsumption architecture. His Genghis robot, for example, now in the Smithsonian Air and Space Museum, used fifty-seven behaviours arranged into a subsumption architecture to control a six-legged mobile robot, which would have been incredibly difficult, if not impossible, to build using knowledge-based AI techniques. These developments moved robotics back into the centre of AI, after many years on the outside.

CHAPTER EIGHT

A complete agent and AI assistants

Before long, it became clear that while behavioural AI had raised important questions about the beliefs on which AI was based, it, too, had serious limitations. The problem was that the technology could not be easily expanded. If all you want to do is to build a robot to vacuum an apartment, then behavioural AI is enough. A vacuum-cleaning robot does not have to reason, or talk in English, or solve complex problems. But it is hard to design behavioural systems with more than just a few behaviours, because you cannot **predict** how they will interact without trying them first, which takes time and money. As efficient as the solutions developed with a behavioural approach were, they generally only solved very narrow problems, which could not easily be applied to others.

Some scientists accepted the key lessons of behavioural AI, but argued that a combination of behavioural and reasoning approaches was required. So, AI activity began to move away from AI theory like expert systems and logical reasoning towards building independent and autonomous agents, doing tasks for a user in a particular environment. An agent was supposed to provide a linked group of capabilities, rather than a single capability like logical reasoning. By concentrating on building complete intelligent agents, rather than just the different intelligent parts, it was hoped that AI could avoid being based on the incorrect beliefs that had so annoyed Brooks.

Behavioural AI had directly affected agent-based AI, but there was now a softer message. By the mid-1990s AI scientists had agreed on three key capabilities for agents.

Firstly, they had to be able to react to their environment, and fit their behaviour to changes in it. Secondly, they had to be able to systematically work to achieve a given task for their user. Finally, agents needed to be social, able not just to talk to other agents, but to work with them on tasks when required.

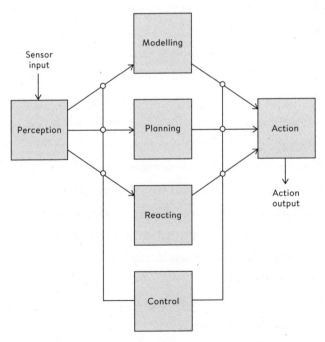

TouringMachines – the typical design of an agent

A typical design for an agent, called **TouringMachines**, divided control into three smaller sub-systems. The reactive sub-system worked like Brooks' subsumption architecture and was responsible for situations that required a quick response and no reasoning, such as avoiding obstacles. The planning sub-system was responsible for working out how to achieve the agent's goals. The modelling sub-system handled **interactions** with other agents. The three control sub-systems were linked by another control sub-system, which listened to what each one suggested and then decided which to follow. This was often a very simple decision, such as: if the reactive sub-system says "STOP!", then you should listen.

Many such agent designs were developed in the early 1990s, including HOMER, a simulated robot which worked in the sea and was given tasks to do, like collecting parcels and moving them from one place to another. Like SHRDLU it was only a **simulation**, but HOMER was much more complex. It took instructions, using about 800 words in English, from a user. It could plan how to achieve and then perform its tasks, changing them as the situation required. To get an idea of its capabilities, here is an example of a conversation with HOMER:

> **Human:** What is in front of you?
> **HOMER:** A log.
> **Human:** Do you own the log?
> **HOMER:** No, I don't.
> **Human:** The log belongs to you.

HOMER: Oh. (Used by HOMER to show it has been told something it did not know previously.)

[. . .]

Human: Turn away from your log.

HOMER: OK, I am turning.

(Log is moved by the user.)

Human: Turn around.

HOMER: OK, I'm turning.

HOMER: I've lost the log!

This dialogue shows HOMER reasoning in a simple but sensible way. It remembered the log, expecting to see it when it turned around, and was surprised to discover that the log had disappeared. The next scenario starts with HOMER waiting at a port to collect a parcel and deliver it to a boat.

Human: Drop the parcel on the boat next Saturday at 9 p.m.

HOMER: OK.

(HOMER creates plan.)

Human: Are you going to the port next Saturday?

HOMER: Yes.

Human: Why are you going to the port?

HOMER: I'll go to the port in order to pick up the parcel.

Human: What time are you going to pick it up?

HOMER: 8.56 p.m.

> **Human:** Where will the parcel be next Sunday?
> **HOMER:** On the boat.
> **Human:** Will the parcel be at the port a week from now?
> **HOMER:** No.

Here we see HOMER showing some understanding of time, and how its actions affect its environment: after it has left the parcel on the boat, the parcel will no longer be at the port. It also shows an understanding that its own plans will take time: it needs to leave the port at 8.56 p.m. to be at the boat for 9 p.m.

Although agent-based AI had its origins in robotics, many researchers quickly realized that it had useful applications in the software world. The big idea was to build AI-powered **software agents** that would work with us to do everyday tasks on personal computers and on the internet. To understand how this idea developed we need to know how we interact with computers, and how thinking on this subject has changed over time.

Users of the earliest computers were, like Alan Turing, very often the scientists and engineers who had helped to design and build them. The **interfaces** to the computers they built were basic, with nothing hidden from the user, who had to understand how the machine worked in order to program it. Very few people had the technical skills to program in this way, and any skills you acquired on one computer would be of no use in programming another because they were completely different machines.

By the end of the 1950s, this situation had begun to change through the development of **high-level programming**

languages. These hid some of the low-level machine details, so a programmer no longer needed to understand how a particular computer worked in order to program it. They were also machine independent, which meant that a program written in COBOL on one computer worked on another computer, and more people could use them.

This change continued and in 1984 the Apple Computer company's Macintosh ("Mac") computer was the first computer produced and sold explicitly to users without specialist training. Its main selling point was its graphical user interface (GUI), with little pictures called icons on the screen **representing** documents and files, all controlled by a computer mouse. Desktop-based graphical user interfaces like that used in the 1984 Mac have changed very little in computers used today.

By the end of the 1980s, Apple was working on the next big change in human-computer interaction and came up with an idea called the Knowledge Navigator, an early **World Wide Web**, which at that time lay a couple of years in the future. This agent-based interface represented a completely different way of interacting with computers. When you use an application like Microsoft Word, it does something because you selected an item, or clicked on a button, making you the only agent in the interaction. The agent-based interface changed that. Instead of the computer waiting to be told what to do, an agent would take an active role, in the same way that a human might. By the middle of the 1990s, interest in software agents grew quickly, thanks to the expansion of the World Wide Web. But search tools were still too simple, and internet connections too slow, for many everyday computer tasks to be automated.

In 2011, an app called Siri appeared, developed for the Apple iPhone at SRI International, the same organisation that had developed SHAKEY thirty years earlier. Siri was a software agent that users could interact with in natural language, and which could do simple tasks for them. Other similar software agents quickly followed: Amazon's Alexa, Google's Assistant and Microsoft's Cortana. They were all developed from agent-based AI, but could not have been built in the 1990s because the technology was not available at the time. They needed the computer power that became available on mobile **devices** from 2010 onwards.

CHAPTER NINE

Towards multi-agent systems

Building agents that can act effectively for humans provided yet another way of thinking about AI, but also raised an interesting question. The Turing test established the idea that the goal of AI was to produce behaviour that was the same as that of humans. But if we want agents to act and do the best for us, it is not important whether they make the same choices as us, simply that they make the best choices possible. So, the goal of AI began to change from building agents that make human choices to agents that make the best choices. The theory behind this, called optimal decision-making, goes back to the 1940s and the important work of John von Neumann and Oskar Morgenstern, in developing a mathematical theory of **rational** or logical decision-making. In agent-based AI, the idea was that the agent would use their theory to make the best, or optimal, decisions for you. The starting point of their theory is your **preferences**. If your agent is to act for you, then it needs to know what you want. You then need the agent to act to deliver your preferred choices as best it can. So, how do we give an agent our preferences?

Suppose your agent has to choose between getting an apple, orange or pear. If your agent is going to do its best for you, then it needs to know your desires. For example, your preferences might be:

- oranges are preferred to pears;
- pears are preferred to apples.

In this case, if your agent were given a choice between an apple and an orange, and chose an orange, you would be happy – if it gave you an apple, you would be disappointed. This is a simple example of a **preference relation**, which describes how you grade every pair of different results.

Von Neumann and Morgenstern required preference relations to be **consistent**.

For example, suppose you said your preferences were:

- oranges are preferred to pears;
- pears are preferred to apples;
- apples are preferred to oranges.

Your preferences are rather odd this time, because the fact that you prefer oranges to pears and pears to apples would lead to the conclusion that you preferred oranges above apples, when the opposite is in fact true. Your preferences are therefore **inconsistent**, making it impossible for an agent to make a good decision for you. The next step is to see that consistent preferences can be represented as numbers, called **utilities**; the larger the number, the more preferred the result.

So, for the first example, we could say that the utility of an orange is 3, the utility of a pear is 2 and the utility of an apple is 1. Since 3 is bigger than 2 and 2 is bigger than 1, these utilities correctly capture our first preference relation. But this does not work when the preferences are inconsistent.

The aim of using utility values to represent preferences is to reduce the problem of making the best choice to a mathematical calculation. Our agent chooses an action with the best result for us, in what we call an optimization problem. But most choices are more complex than this because they involve uncertainty. Settings of choice under uncertainty deal with scenarios where actions have several possible results, and all we know about them is how likely they are to happen.

Let's look at a scenario in which your agent has to make a choice between two actions.

- Choice 1: A coin is thrown. If it lands showing side A your agent is given £4. If it shows side B your agent is given £3.
- Choice 2: A coin is thrown. If it lands showing side A your agent is given £6. If it shows side B your agent is given nothing.

Which choice should your agent make? Choice 1 is better, but why? We need to understand something called **expected utility**, the utility, or in this case amount, that would be received on average from that scenario.

For choice 1, we would expect sides A and B of the coin to appear, on average, an equal number of times: half the time your agent would receive £4, and half the time it would receive £3. So, the expected utility from choice 1 and the amount of money you would receive on average would be: $(0.5 \times £4) + (0.5 \times £3) = £3.50$.

Following the same reasoning, the expected utility of choice 2 is on average: $(0.5 \times £6) + (0.5 \times £0) = £3$.

Now, the basic idea in von Neumann and Morgenstern's theory says that a rational agent would choose to get the biggest expected utility, in this case, choice 1. This is despite the fact that you could get £6 if you chose 2; you would be just as likely to get nothing. Some people do not like the idea of reducing human choices to mathematical calculations, but this simply captures preferences in numbers, nothing more. By the 1990s, building agents that would act logically for us, according to this model, had become normal in AI, and still is today.

From 2000 on, researchers began to wonder if software agents could talk to each other. The idea was not completely new, as back in the days of knowledge-based AI, researchers had developed languages that would allow expert systems to share knowledge and ask each other questions. But this new idea, **multi-agent systems**, was different in one important way:

I want my agent to go out and do the best it can for me; you want your agent to go out and do the best it can for you; but my desires and preferences are probably not the same as yours, and so neither will those of our agents be. Our agents are going to need the kind of social abilities that we all use in the everyday world to interact with each other.

The new challenge for AI was to build agents that had these capabilities. It seems odd now that these social aspects of AI had not been considered sooner, but, before the development of multi-agent systems, researchers had been concentrating on developing individual agents, without worrying about how they might interact with other AI agents. The possibility that there could be many agents, rather than just one, greatly changed the AI story. The problem an agent has to solve is that of knowing what action to perform for a user. But if there are many agents around, whether the action chosen by an agent is good or not will probably depend, at least in part, on what other agents choose to do. An agent should therefore consider what these other agents are likely to do when making its decision. This kind of reasoning had in fact been previously studied in the field of game theory, the part of economics that studies decision-making. As the name suggests, game theory was originally developed from the study of games like chess, and has applications everywhere that decisions are to be made in the presence of many agents.

By the end of the 1990s, we built agents that considered our preferences, acted for us logically and used the rational decision-making developed in expected utility theory. These agents used their understanding of the world, and if there were many agents, we looked to game theory to provide the basic shape for making decisions. It was not General AI, and it did not give any instructions for how to get to it. But by developing and accepting these tools, the AI world became a recognized scientific field, no longer searching in the dark.

There were two important achievements in this period which supported this. The first made news around the world. In 1997, the company IBM was able to show that an AI system, called

DeepBlue, could **consistently** beat Russian chess champion Garry Kasparov. Chess became a solved game for AI from this point on, thanks to two main ingredients: heuristic search, which we first heard about in Chapter Five; and enormous computer power, which some people argued was not AI at all.

While you may well have heard about DeepBlue beating Kasparov, it is unlikely that you will have heard of the second big AI achievement of the time. NP-complete problems, which we also first heard about in Chapter Five, are problems that are very hard to find answers to. By the early 1990s, it was beginning to be clear that progress on algorithms for NP-complete problems meant that they were no longer such an obstacle to AI. The first problem shown to be NP-complete was called SAT (short for "satisfiability"). This is the problem of checking whether a simple logical expression is consistent, whether it could be true. SAT is the most basic of all NP-complete problems, but remember that if you solve just one problem you could solve them all.

By the end of the 1990s, "SAT solvers" – programs to solve SAT problems – were powerful enough that they began to be used on industrial-size problems. They are now regularly used in computing as another tool for dealing with NP-complete problems. This does not mean that they can always be solved efficiently, but it is an incredible achievement for AI.

CHAPTER TEN

Machine learning

The goal of machine learning is programs that can calculate a desired **output** from data **input**, without being given an explicit recipe for how to do this. A typical application for machine learning is text recognition: turning handwritten text into typed text. This is hard, as we all write in different and often unclear ways, and our pens lose ink on the paper, which makes it damaged and dirty. Text recognition is not like playing board games, where we have recipes that work in theory but need heuristics to make them practical. We just do not know what a recipe for text recognition might be. This is where machine learning comes in.

A machine learning program for text recognition would typically be trained by giving it many examples of handwritten numbers or letters, each with a label of the actual typed text. This kind of machine learning is called **supervised learning** and requires a lot of carefully chosen **training** data to be successful.

Programs are usually trained with only a tiny percentage of the possible inputs and outputs, as we cannot show all the possible handwritten inputs. If we could, there would be no need for any machine learning techniques, as whenever our program was presented with an input it would just look up the matching output. For machine learning, a program must be trained with only a small part of the total collection of training data. However, if the amount of data is too small, it may not provide enough information for the program to learn the right **mapping** from inputs to outputs.

Another basic problem with training data is **feature extraction**. Suppose you work for a bank, which wants a machine learning program to identify customers who are unsafe to lend money to – bad credit **risks**. The training data will probably provide lots of records of past customers, each with a good-risk or bad-risk label on them. The record will typically include a name, date of birth, address, income and information about money paid in and out of the customer's bank account. But which **features** do you need to include in your training data? Some will be more important than others. If you include everything, this could lead to a problem called the curse of dimensionality. This means that the more features you include, the more training data you need to give the program. And the program will learn more slowly. However, if you only include a small number of features in your training data, you may accidentally leave out features needed to allow the program to learn correctly; those that actually show a bad credit risk. If, for example, the only feature that you decided to include for your bad-risk program was the customer's address, then this is likely to lead to a program **bias** against people living in certain areas.

In **reinforcement learning**, we do not give the program any explicit training data: it experiments by making decisions, and receives reports about them. For example, reinforcement learning is widely used to train programs to play games. The program plays the game, and gets a positive report if it wins or a negative report if it loses. Whether positive or negative, the report is called the **reward**, and considered by the program next time it plays. A positive reward would make it more likely to play the same way again; a negative reward, less likely to do so.

A key difficulty with reinforcement learning is that rewards may take a long time to come, making it hard for the program to know which actions were good and which were bad. Suppose our reinforcement-learning program loses a game; how does it or we know *when* it moved badly?

One of the oldest and most successful machine learning techniques in AI is neural nets. This is based on the 100 billion **neurons**, each with thousands of connections, in the human brain, and the idea is to make the same kind of system in a computer program, so that it can learn like a human brain.

In the 1940s, US researchers Warren McCulloch and Walter Pitts realized that neurons could be modelled as electrical circuits, or simple logical circuits. They used this idea to develop a basic but very general mathematical model. This model was improved in the 1950s by Frank Rosenblatt in the first neural net model to be actually used, called the **perceptron model**.

In the perceptron model, each input has a number called its weight (W), and each input to the neuron is either active or inactive. If an input is active, then it "**stimulates**" the neuron by the **corresponding** weight; and each neuron has an **activation threshold**, which is another number (T). If the neuron is stimulated beyond its activation threshold (T), then it will make its output active. So if the total weights of all the inputs that are active is the same or bigger than T, then the neuron produces an output.

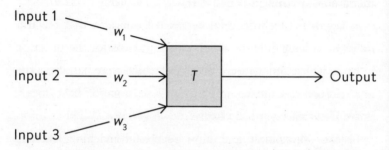

A single neural unit in Rosenblatt's perceptron model

Of course, the neural nets that we see in nature contain many neurons, connecting in many different ways, so more complex perceptron models were developed. But research mostly concentrated on networks with a single layer, as nobody had any idea how to train neural networks with more than one layer. Rosenblatt found a technique for training neural networks to find the right weights and correctly **map** inputs to outputs for a simple perceptron model, which he called an error correction procedure. Although his approach always works, single-layer perceptron networks are limited as they often cannot learn even simple relationships between inputs and outputs. Perceptrons with many layers do not have such limitations, but they remained only theory until twenty years later.

A 1980s book called *Parallel Distributed Processing* (or PDP, for short)[5] changed this. It showed how to find out what the "weights" of the connections between neurons should be in neural nets with many layers. The solution was an algorithm called **backpropagation**, or backprop; probably the single most important technique in the field of neural nets. Backprop works by looking at cases where a neural net has made an error in **classification**, which appears at the output layer of the network. Imagine the network has been shown a picture of a cat, and the output layer has **classified** it as a dog. The backprop algorithm propagates the error backwards through each previous layer of the network, in a process called gradient descent. First it maps the errors for each possible weight, then finds the sharpest drop in all stages of the map, from the present error down to the lowest error of all. This provides the fastest way to deal with the error.

While PDP and backprop made a lot of new applications possible for neural nets, by the mid-1990s progress had once again slowed because of the limitations of computers of that time, and other areas of machine learning seemed to be making fast progress.

The big idea that drove the third stage of neural net research was called **deep learning**. Deep neural networks have more layers, and more better-connected neurons. But two further ingredients were required to make deep learning a success: data and computer power.

The importance of data to machine learning can be seen in the story of the ImageNet project, the idea of a Chinese-born researcher, Fei Fei Li, working at the AI lab at Stanford from 2013 to 2018. Li decided that deep learning needed large, well-kept data collections, against which new systems could be trained, tested and compared. So she started the ImageNet project, a large online collection of what is now about 14 million digital photographs which have been carefully classified into 22,000 different groups, using an online dictionary called WordNet. This contains a large number of words classified, for example, as words that mean the same or opposite, and so on. An important moment for image classification came in 2012, when British-Canadian researcher Geoff Hinton and his team showed a system called AlexNet, a neural net that greatly improved image recognition in an international competition. But the final ingredient required to make deep learning work was computer-processing power. A new type of **computer processor**, Graphics Processing Units (GPUs), originally developed to deal with graphics problems in computer games, proved perfect for training neural nets.

But for all their success, deep learning and neural nets still have limitations. The expert opinion of a neural network lies in its weights, corresponding to the links between neurons. As yet, we have no way of approaching or understanding this knowledge. A deep learning program that identifies an illness cannot explain its diagnosis; a deep learning program which decides not to lend money to a customer cannot tell you why it does so. Another key problem for deep learning is that it does not always work. It is possible to make small changes to images, which humans cannot see, but which lead to neural nets wrongly classifying them. Much more work is needed on the study of this issue known as **adversarial machine learning**, as it could be very serious if, for example, a program in a driverless car were to wrongly classify road signs.

CHAPTER ELEVEN

DeepMind and beyond

DeepMind is the perfect example of the rise of deep learning. When Google bought DeepMind in 2014 for £400,000,000, it was a small AI company employing fewer than twenty-five people, which did not seem to have any products, technology or a business plan; just the aim of solving intelligence. DeepMind had actually trained a program to play forty-nine Atari video games from the early 1980s. To understand the importance of this achievement, you have to know what the program did and did not do. The only information it was given was the image that would appear on the screen and the present score of the game. The results were incredible: the program taught itself to play twenty-nine of the forty-nine games at above human-level, with super-human levels on some games.

People were particularly interested in a game called *Breakout*, one of the first video games. The player controls a "bat" which is used to hit a "ball" against a wall of coloured "bricks". The goal is to destroy the whole wall as quickly as possible. After playing the game hundreds of times, the program became expert, learning that the best way to quickly get a good score was to make a hole through the wall. Nobody told the program to do this, so this behaviour took the developers totally by surprise.

The main technique used in the Atari player was reinforcement learning, playing again and again, applied using a neural network with three hidden layers. The inputs to the neural network were pre-processed, having reduced the image size and replaced the colour with shades of grey. The program took a small number of its available inputs, only using every fourth image. The neural network was trained using typical deep learning techniques.

But the program was not perfect, performing very badly with some games, such as *Montezuma's Revenge*. Unlike *Breakout*, where the reward follows almost immediately, in *Montezuma's Revenge* the player has to carry out a complex sequence of tasks before getting a reward.

DeepMind followed this success with many more, the most famous being AlphaGo, a program to play Go, a very old Chinese board game. The rules of Go are much simpler than chess, yet in 2015, Go-playing programs performed well below the level of human experts. This is because Go has a much larger board than chess and a larger branching factor.

As basic search techniques cannot deal with these issues, something else is required. AlphaGo used two neural networks: the value network estimated how good a given board position was; while the policy network gave advice about how to move, based on the board position. The policy network contained thirteen layers, and was trained by using supervised learning first, where the training data was examples of games played by expert humans; and then reinforcement learning, based on self-play. Finally, these two networks were built into a complex search technique, called Monte Carlo tree search.

In March 2016, when AlphaGo played against Lee Sedol, a world champion Go player, AlphaGo won four games to one. People were extremely interested in the match, but noticed that the program seemed to move in a way that a human would not, and could not really understand. AlphaGo cannot tell us why it moves as it does, which is one of the key challenges with deep learning. And although seen as a success for the new AI of deep learning and big data, on careful examination it is a lot like the AI search developed in Arthur Samuel's checkers-playing program, discussed in Chapter Five.

Before long DeepMind was in the news again, this time with AlphaGo Zero, a program that learned how to play Go to a super-human level without any human supervision, just by playing against itself. Yet another system, called AlphaZero, learned to play a range of other games, including chess. After just nine hours of self-play, AlphaZero was able to consistently beat or draw against Stockfish, one of the world's leading chess-playing programs. It was exciting that AlphaZero could play many different types of board games, but it still did not have anything like the general intelligent capabilities that humans have. It plays board games brilliantly, but it cannot chat, make a joke, cook a meal, or ride a bicycle. Its amazing abilities are still very narrow; and of course, board games are a long way from the real world. Despite this, DeepMind's work represented an extraordinary series of achievements in AI.

You can see the limitations of deep learning techniques in two widely used applications: image captioning and automated translation. In an image-captioning problem, you want a computer to take an image and describe it through text. Systems with some capability are now widely used. These include a photo-management application in Apple Mac software that classifies your pictures as "Beach", "Party", and so on. There are also several websites, typically run by international research groups, which attempt to describe the photos you have saved. For example, Microsoft's CaptionBot can correctly identify a key element of a picture and recognize where it is but cannot really understand the picture.

Machine learning systems like CaptionBot are trained by giving them a very large number of training examples, each one **consisting** of a picture with a text label. Eventually, after being shown enough pictures with the right label, perhaps of a famous actor, the system is able to correctly name the actor whenever it sees their picture. This is a very useful capability with lots of possible applications, but the program does not recognize the actor or what is happening in the picture in any meaningful way. Not only do such systems have a limited ability to understand the pictures they are shown, they have no understanding of the picture as humans would have, from lived experiences of the world. This does not mean that AI systems cannot show understanding, but rather that understanding means more than being able to map a certain input (a picture containing an actor) to a certain output (the text with the actor's name).

Automated translation between different languages is another area in which deep learning has led to quick progress in recent years. Google Translate is probably the best-known program. Originally made available as a product in 2006, the most recent program uses deep learning and neural nets. The system is trained by giving it large amounts of translated texts. But, when it tries to translate the complex language from a twentieth-century novel such as "In Search of Lost Time", by the French author Marcel Proust, its success is limited. It translates the text in an unnatural way, using strange sentences which are difficult to understand. The reason for this is that, to translate the work successfully, the program would also need a lot of knowledge about French society and life at the time, as well as French history and culture. A neural net like that used in Google Translate has none of this knowledge.

This problem is not new to AI. The Cyc project described in Chapter Six experienced similar difficulties. Deep learning will probably be part of the solution, but it will require something more than just a larger neural net, or more processing power, or more training data from French novels. It will require new developments as incredible as deep learning itself to connect the world of explicitly represented knowledge with the world of deep learning and neural nets.

CHAPTER TWELVE

AI today

AI is now present in all areas of our lives: education, science, industry, business, farming, healthcare, free time, the media, arts and beyond. In April 2019, scientists used AI to take the first ever pictures of a black hole, an area of space with such powerful energy that nothing can escape it. The incredible image was only possible through the advanced computer vision algorithms used to predict the missing parts of the picture.

In 2018, researchers from tech company Nvidia showed fake pictures of people which looked totally real, developed by a new type of neural network, a generative adversarial network, which will be a key tool in future **virtual reality**. And at the end of 2018 DeepMind researchers presented AlphaFold, a system to help treat serious medical conditions like Alzheimer's disease, using machine learning techniques to predict future signs of the disease.

Money for healthcare was a problem in the 1980s as it is now, so MYCIN (discussed in Chapter Six) was followed by other mostly **theoretical** expert systems. Personal healthcare management has now become possible thanks to wearable devices, which check how fast your heart is beating or your body temperature. These already give us health advice and goals, and perhaps in future they will be able to identify symptoms of disease, or even call an ambulance. Powerful personal computers, like our smartphones, only require simple AI techniques, constantly connected to the internet, and linked to wearable devices with a range of physical sensors. Some applications may only need a basic smartphone. Researchers at the University of Oxford believe that changes in people's behaviour recorded by their phone could **diagnose** dementia, a disease of the brain often affecting old people, long before there are any other signs or a formal diagnosis.

The problem is that wearable technology creates a lot of personal data, which can help you but can also be misused. In 2016, the health insurance company Vitality started offering its customers Apple Watches, then changed their insurance costs depending on how much exercise they took.

Automated diagnosis is another exciting AI application we could soon see in healthcare. Machine learning is perfect for understanding data from medical devices. In 2018, DeepMind explained how they were working with London's Moorfields Eye Hospital to develop techniques to automatically identify eye problems. The system used two neural networks: the first trained on about 900 images, showing how a human expert would identify the parts of the image; the second trained on about 15,000 examples for diagnosis. The results were excellent, showing that the system performed at, or above, the level of human experts.

Despite the evidence showing that we can now build systems that can achieve human expert performance in examining medical data, some people think we should be careful about doing so. Real human professionals are still needed to interact with their patients and fully understand their conditions.

Another argument against using AI in healthcare is that some people do not trust machines, even though they can make diagnoses that are as good as those of human experts. But even the most experienced humans make mistakes, and we all show bias, and often are not very good at logical decision-making. The challenge in healthcare is not to replace human healthcare workers with AI, but to use it to help them. AI could have the greatest social effect in making expert systems available to people in parts of the world where no healthcare is available.

———————

Every year more than a million people die, and 50 million are injured, in road accidents internationally. AI could greatly reduce this, saving lives through driverless cars. They would also be cheaper, more efficient and more environmentally friendly. We might not even need to own cars any more if there were enough cheap driverless taxis around. There is a long history of research in this area, but the technology for driverless cars only really became possible in the 1970s. The challenge was huge, and the key problem was perception. If you could find a way for a car to know precisely where it was and what was around it, then you would have solved the problem of driverless cars. The solution was modern machine learning techniques, without which driverless cars would not be possible.

The PROMETHEUS project is widely seen to have led to today's driverless car technology. In 1995, a car drove itself from Munich in Germany to Odense in Denmark and back, with human **interventions** required on average every five and a half miles, and the longest distance without human intervention was about a hundred miles. This was all the more amazing because of the limited computer power available at the time. Although PROMETHEUS was not a fully finished car, the project signalled that this technology could eventually be sold to the public.

Thanks to the 2005 Grand Challenge, a competition for driverless cars held by DARPA, a US military organization, driverless cars became a solved problem and one of the great technological achievements in human history. This was followed by other challenges, including the 2007 Urban Challenge, when driverless cars had to obey Californian road traffic laws, and manage everyday situations like parking, crossings and traffic. Six teams successfully completed the challenge, with the winner, from Carnegie Mellon University, averaging about 14 miles per hour during the four-hour challenge. Since then, there has been a huge amount of money put into the technology from well-known car companies afraid of being left behind, and from newer companies wanting to take the lead.

In 2014 the US Society of Automotive Engineers provided a useful car autonomy classification model as shown on the following page:

Level 0: No autonomy: The car has no automated controls. The driver is in complete control of the car at all times (although the car may warn the driver or give them other data). Most cars on the roads today are Level 0.

Level 1: Driver assistance: The car takes some control from the driver, for example through an adaptive cruise control system, which can keep the car's speed the same, but the driver must pay complete attention.

Level 2: Partial **automation**: The car takes control of how fast and how it moves, although the driver is still expected to continually check the roads and be ready to **intervene** if necessary.

Level 3: Conditional automation: The human driver is no longer expected to be continually checking the road, although the car may ask the user to take control if it finds a situation that it cannot manage.

Level 4: High automation: The car normally takes control, although the driver can still intervene.

Level 5: Full automation: The dream of driverless cars: you get in a car, give your destination, and the car does everything.

Probably the best driverless car technology you can buy today is Tesla's Autopilot, which is about level 2. A key problem seems to be that drivers trust the available technology too much. At Level 0 and Level 5 it is clear what is expected of the driver, but between these two levels it is not clear what drivers must expect to do. An accident in Arizona in March 2018 raised these doubts, when a driverless car owned by Uber hit and killed a person. The car was travelling too fast, so by the time the car recognized it needed to stop it was too late. Although the car's sensors perceived an "obstacle", in this case a person in the road, the software seems to have been designed to avoid stopping suddenly. Most importantly, the "safety driver" in the car appears to have been watching TV on her smartphone, and not the road. So, a human rather than a technological mistake led to the terrible death of Elaine Herzberg, which could have been avoided.

Given all these facts, we probably will not see totally driverless cars on our streets for another twenty years. The key difficulty is dealing with unexpected events. We can train cars to deal with most routine and expected scenarios, but there are lots of situations which are impossible to predict. A human driver would deal with them through their experience of the world, which driverless cars do not have and will not have in the near future.

Another big problem is how to move from mostly human-driven cars on the road, through a mixed scenario (some human-driven, some driverless cars), to a completely driverless future. Driverless cars can confuse and frighten the human drivers they share the roads with; while human drivers do not always follow the rules, making it hard for AI software to predict their behaviour and interact with them safely.

The solution might be to use the technology in "safe" areas, without many people, before gradually moving into the wider world. Many industries already use the technology in places such as Western Australia. Factories, ports and military areas could follow this model in the next few years.

Beyond this, low-speed driverless taxis could be used for well-mapped city roads. In fact, several companies are testing such services in a limited way now, with human "safety drivers" in the cars for emergencies.

Finally, we could also keep driverless cars to one lane on roads, helped by sensors and other technology, much as we already have bus and cycle lanes.

CHAPTER THIRTEEN

What could go wrong with AI

The fast progress in AI since the beginning of this century has led to many media stories supporting the idea that we are creating something we will not be able to control, and that could be harmful to us. In modern AI this is often linked to an idea called the **Singularity**: a theoretical point at which computer intelligence goes beyond that of humans, when computers start to use their own intelligence to improve themselves. This process would continue until it became impossible for human intelligence to regain control of it.

However, if we stop to think about the logic behind the Singularity, it is based on the idea that computer **hardware** is developing at such a speed that the information-processing capacity of computers will soon be greater than that of the human brain. This argument is linked to a well-known rule in computing: Moore's **law** says that computer processors can be expected to have double the power every eighteen months. So we could conclude that their power would get cheaper at the same speed, and the processors themselves smaller.

But, like computers, AI has limitations. Software, such as machine learning programs, improves at a much slower speed than the hardware. And even if AI systems did become as intelligent as people, they would not necessarily be able to improve themselves at a speed beyond our ability to understand. Progress on AI has been slow, and at present there is no path that will take us to the Singularity.

Despite this, enough people are worried about AI to make it worth thinking seriously about ways to control its development.

———————

The Three Laws of Robotics were created by well-known author Isaac Asimov in a series of stories about robots with a kind of strong AI. These laws were:

1. A robot may not injure a human or, through inaction, allow a human to come to harm.

2. A robot must obey orders given by humans except where they would be against the First Law.

3. A robot must protect itself, as long as this is not against the First or Second Laws.

Could we build AI systems with such laws built in? Apart from the difficulty of not going against the First and Second Laws, their use for AI systems is impractical. Every time an AI system was thinking about an action, it would need to consider the effects that this action might have on *all* humans, now and in the future. The idea of "harm" is difficult, too. When you fly, you are using a lot of energy and creating a lot of pollution, which causes harm. A robot that obeyed Asimov's laws could never fly, or do many other things that could cause harm. So, Asimov's laws might provide good general rules for AI systems, but they could never be built into them.

So how should we think about controlling the behaviour of AI systems?

The Trolley Problem is a scenario which has recently attracted a lot of attention applied to AI, because we might soon have driverless cars. It is an **ethics** problem about a trolley, or tram, out of control, travelling at high speed towards five people, who are unable to move. If you pull a handle, the trolley will go down a different track, and kill just one person (who cannot move either), saving the other five. Should you pull the handle or not?

Although it seems simple, the Trolley Problem raises some surprisingly complex issues. Would it be better to let just one person die rather than five? Philosophers call this kind of reasoning **consequentialist**, because it decides on the ethics of actions based on their **consequences**, or results. The best known consequentialist theory is called utilitarianism, from the work of eighteenth-century British philosophers Jeremy Bentham and John Stuart Mill. They created the idea of the "greatest happiness principle", which says that one should act for the greatest good for society. It seems attractive until you apply it to the Trolley Problem. What if the five people were really evil, while the single person was an innocent young child? Which lives have more value?

A different way of considering the Trolley Problem is to follow a general rule of "good" actions. In practice this means not taking any action, because taking any life is wrong, even though not acting leads to five other deaths. While yet another idea is that of virtue ethics, which says we might identify a decision-maker with good ethics and try to act like they would in the situation.

Of course, in AI, the decision-maker would be an agent, a driverless car, which must choose between driving straight ahead and killing five people, or changing direction and killing one. So, what should an AI agent do when dealing with such a problem?

Firstly, it is not reasonable to expect an AI system to solve a problem the greatest philosophical thinkers in the world cannot agree on. Secondly, human drivers are not expected to pass ethics exams, and the Trolley Problem is not usually a big part of driving a car, so why should AI systems have to solve it? Thirdly, there is no single answer, as there are big differences in **ethical** decision-making, not only between different people, but in different parts of the world. When dealing with a situation like the Trolley Problem, a real driverless car would probably try to improve safety and avoid danger, without any deep reasoning, and simply stop.

One of the first and most important systems of ethical AI was the Asilomar principles, twenty-three rules created by a group of AI scientists in Asilomar, California. Most of the rules were easy to agree to: AI research should create intelligence for good purposes; AI systems should be safe; people should have the right to get, manage and control their own data in AI systems. But some rules seemed harder: the money created by AI should be shared and used for the good of everyone; which is fine for research, but big businesses want to make money, not save the world. Finally, there are rules considering how to keep control of AI in future, which seem to concentrate on the wrong issues.

Among the many different ethical systems suggested, there seem to be three main similarities according to Virginia Dignum at Umeå University in Sweden[6]. The first is accountability, which means that if an AI system makes a decision that affects someone, then that person has a right to an explanation of that decision. But as we have already seen, machine learning programs are not capable of explaining the reasons for their decisions at present.

The second is **responsibility**, or making it clear who is responsible for a decision – not the AI system, but the people or organizations that created it. This introduces the issue of moral agency, the ability to identify right from wrong, and understand the effects of actions. It is easy to imagine that AI systems can be moral agents, but software is not answerable for its actions. Responsibility in AI is not about building machines that are responsible, but about developing AI systems in a responsible way. A Siri-like software agent that made users think they were interacting with a real person would be an irresponsible use of AI by the developers; the software is not to blame, those who develop it are.

Thirdly, **transparency** means that we should be able to get to our data on an AI system, and understand any algorithms used within it.

Talk of ethical AI can make us forget the true but boring fact that AI software can go wrong, like any new technology. For AI software to work, we need to tell it what we want it to do for us. This is often not as easy as it might appear. It is impossible to tell a program what we want if we do not actually know ourselves. And how is an AI system to understand our desires if they are inconsistent? How should an AI system fill in the missing information if we can only give it an incomplete picture of our preferences? Finally, we do not usually explicitly tell people our values and beliefs because we imagine they are shared, but an AI system will not know them unless we tell it or make sure that they are already built into it.

One way of getting an AI system to achieve our goals is to tell it to keep everything in the world as close to how it is now as possible. For example, if we give the instruction "Stop anyone breaking into my house", what we mean is "Stop anyone breaking into my house, while keeping everything else as close to how it is now as possible". So burning the house down is not a way to achieve this goal. To do this we need to let a machine learning program see what a human does, and try to learn a reward system from what it sees, looking to human behaviour as a model for desirable behaviour. This is called inverse reinforcement learning.

CHAPTER FOURTEEN
How AI will affect our lives

Although the Singularity might not arrive any time soon, that does not mean that there is nothing to fear from AI. As a general-purpose technology, AI can be misused or have unintended consequences – its applications are limited only by our imagination. One of the things people worry most about is how AI will affect the future of work, and if it will cause unemployment. Computers do not get tired, turn up to work late, argue, or complain, and they are not paid. It is easy to see why employers are interested, and workers are nervous.

This is nothing new. Machines have gradually replaced humans in many industries, changing the work people do and the places where they do it. New technologies have created more jobs and wealth than have been destroyed. But while automation in the past took the jobs of unskilled workers, perhaps AI will take skilled jobs from workers. And if it does, which jobs will be left for people?

A 2013 report[7] by researchers at the University of Oxford predicted that office or factory jobs, and jobs involving the movement of people or things, might all be in danger. However, jobs in the arts, media and science, involving ideas; jobs requiring strong social skills; and jobs requiring perception and **dexterity** would all be safe. Although great progress has been made in machine perception, humans are better able to quickly understand highly complex environments; robots can only deal with organized and regular environments. Similarly, the human hand remains far more **dexterous** than the best robot hand.

While some critics accused the report of being extremely negative about future employment, technology will probably replace people in some jobs in the near future. Particularly if the job involves: looking at data on a form and making a decision, like whether or not to lend money; a controlled customer phone call; or driving around, in a well-mapped area of a city. However, most people will not be replaced by AI systems, they will simply use AI tools that make them better and more efficient at their jobs.

Other people hope that AI, robotics and advanced automation will lead to a very different and freer future. They believe that AI will do the dirty, dangerous, and boring jobs nobody wants; while people write novels, discuss philosophy, or go mountain climbing. This dream is not new. When computer technology was developed in the 1970s and early 1980s, people imagined that they would spend much less time in paid employment and have more free time. One theory is that in fact they worked longer hours to earn more money to pay for more things.

Recent technological developments, particularly in AI, have brought an idea back to people's attention: that everyone in society should receive a certain income. The suggestion is that AI/robotics/automation will create enough wealth to make what is known as **universal basic income** possible (because machines can do the work) and desirable (because robots have taken all the jobs). But for this to be possible, AI would have to make a huge amount of money, and there would need to be political and social support for it; which is unlikely.

The progress in AI technologies has already changed work patterns. Fifty years ago, it was not unusual for people to work for the same company all their lives. Today many people are employed on part-time, casual or short contracts. This is partly due to the rise of mobile computing technology, which makes it possible to coordinate large groups of workers internationally. Employers know where workers are at any given time, they can contact them with instructions and check that they are doing their tasks efficiently, through computer programs.

You could argue that this leaves little room for workers to have great ideas, create new things and be seen as individuals. Imagine how you would feel if a computer program decided how well you were doing your job and even decided whether you should lose it. It is of course important to remember that technology has no opinion about how it is used. Employers, governments and organizations should be thinking about this side of AI and how it could affect workers.

The use of AI not only challenges workers' rights, but human rights, through AI systems that help decide who goes to prison. The UK police in Durham have an AI system called HART (Harm Assessment Risk Tool), which helps police officers make decisions about who should be suspected of a crime. HART is a typical application of machine learning, trained on 104,000 pieces of data. The system has proved to be accurate 98% of the time in low-risk cases; and 88% of the time with high-risk cases, as it was designed to be more careful in cases of violent crimes. Although HART was being used as a support tool to help police officers decide, people still felt uncomfortable about it. One problem was that important decisions were made based on a very narrow group of case features, without the understanding of people and processes that an experienced officer would have. The lack of transparency, typical of machine learning programs unable to explain decisions, was also worrying. The possibility of bias in the training data and the selected features was also raised as an issue (including the use of people's addresses). Finally, although the tool was only supposed to support decision-making, it was thought that it **risked** becoming the main decision-maker at some point in the future, for a tired, confused or lazy officer.

Behind all the problems with systems like HART is the idea that they remove human judgement in society. Many of us feel more comfortable if we know that a human being, not a computer, is making a decision that has serious consequences for another human being. It is worth protecting the basic human rights we fought so hard for in the past. AI tools should be used to support human decision-makers, not replace them. Also, HART was developed by an experienced research team after carefully considering issues that developing such a tool might raise.

But what if this were not always the case?

Military organisations are also extremely interested in the use of AI due to the increased use of drones: aeroplanes, without human pilots, which can carry weapons. Drones can be smaller, lighter and cheaper than normal aeroplanes, and can be used in situations that are too **risky** for pilots. Since 2001, remote-controlled drones, flown from a distance, have been used by the USA in countries like Afghanistan, Pakistan and Yemen, probably hundreds of times; resulting in possibly thousands of deaths. They raise all sorts of serious ethical issues. Since the pilots controlling the drones are in no physical danger, they might choose to take actions that they would not if they were physically present, and they might not take the consequences of their actions as seriously.

The possibility of autonomous drones is even more worrying, as they could act largely without human guidance or intervention, and could even decide whether or not to take human life. A country with autonomous weapons might also take the decision to go to war more easily and more often, without any risk to its people.

Professor Ron Arkin at USA's Georgia Tech University has argued[8] that since someone, somewhere, will eventually build autonomous weapons, we should consider designing them to behave more ethically than human soldiers; although it is unclear how. Other arguments in support of autonomous weapons include the idea it would surely be better to have robots in wars rather than people; the winner being the side with the better robots. And is it ethical to say autonomous weapons are wrong but ordinary weapons are not?

AI-powered autonomous weapons are already possible with today's technology. However, even with public and political support to control or ban the development and use of autonomous weapons that can kill, it might be difficult to make laws about these weapons. The good news is that at least there are signs that governments are willing to try.

CHAPTER FIFTEEN

Things aren't quite what they seem

We might hope that AI systems would be free of the biases of the human world, but that is not the case. As machine learning systems have been applied to more areas, we have begun to understand how automated decision-making systems can show **algorithmic bias**. Two types of harm have been identified and linked to this. Allocative harm is when a particular group is or is not chosen based on some feature. For example, banks might use a machine learning AI system to predict whether someone is going to be a good customer. They might train the program using records of good and bad customers, and after a while, the AI system might be able to look at information about a new customer, and predict if they are likely to be good or bad. If the program is **biased**, then it might not lend money to a certain group, or prefer to lend money to another group. **Representation harm** happens when a system acts to create or increase bias against someone or something. A very horrible example of this type of harm occurred in 2015, when a Google photo classification system put the label "gorillas" on pictures of black people. But as computers are nothing more than machines for following instructions how can they possibly be biased?

The single most important path for bias is through data, which can be biased in various ways. The simplest is when people creating the groups of data have a bias, although it may not be explicit or **conscious**. However balanced and reasonable we might think we are, we all have biases of some kind, which will automatically be included in the training data we create.

Machine learning can accidentally help to create biases, too, if the training data for a machine learning program is not **representative**. Suppose a bank trained its software on data from one geographical area: the program might end up being biased against people from all other areas. Badly designed programs can also be biased. For example, if the key feature of the data that you chose to train your banking program on was the colour of your customers' skin, it would be no surprise if the resulting program made extremely biased decisions about who it should lend money to. Algorithmic bias is a particularly important issue at present because AI systems cannot explain the decisions they make in the way that a person can. This problem is made worse when we trust the systems too much, which seems to be exactly what we do.

Another issue for AI is that it has historically been mostly developed by men. This situation is changing, but there are still more men than women involved in AI. If AI is only designed by men, then we will end up with male AI. This means AI systems which have a particular view of the world, which will not represent or welcome women. This is because of the data gap: the historical data usually used for making and designing things is male. You can see this in offices, which are heated at temperatures to suit men, and you can also see it in more serious things like safety systems in cars which are designed to fit men's bodies.[9]

For AI, of course, data is key and male bias in data is everywhere. Sometimes the bias is explicit, such as in the TIMIT spoken-word data widely used to train speech understanding programs. The data group contains 69% male voices, with the consequence that speech understanding systems do a much worse job of understanding female voices than male ones. But, sometimes, the bias is not as clear. Suppose you collect pictures of kitchens, which generally show women, to train your machine learning program; or suppose that you collect pictures of company bosses, which generally show men. You can imagine the result, but you might not realize that this has actually happened.

Fake news, as the name suggests, is false, inaccurate or misleading information that is presented as fact. The world had plenty of fake news before the digital age, but the internet and, more particularly, social media seem to be the perfect way to spread it, with serious consequences. When social media applications first appeared, they all seemed to be about friends, family and everyday life, and had lots of pictures of children and cats. But they are such a powerful tool, they quickly began to be used for other purposes: to change events at an international level. Fake news came to the world's attention in 2016, thanks to two events: the US elections for President, which led to the election of Donald Trump; and the UK national vote on remaining in or leaving the European Union, which resulted in a narrow win for the leave vote.

In both cases, there were suggestions that social media had been used to spread fake news stories, which helped the winners. AI is an important part of the fake news story because it is key to spreading it. Social media depend on advertising to make money. If you like what you see, then you spend more time on the site. So social media sites do not show you the truth, but show you what you like, which you tell them, every time you press the "Like" button. AI works out your preferences from what you say you like, the comments that you leave, and the links you follow. It then uses these to find new items that you will also like. All companies have teams of researchers and developers working on these AI problems. What makes this so worrying is that social media are changing our beliefs at an international level, either on purpose or accidentally.

In the future, AI may change the way we perceive the world on an even more basic level. Each of us gains information about the world through our sight, hearing, touch, smell and taste, and we use this information to build a widely accepted view of how the world actually is. If you and I both see a particular event in the same way, then we get the same information about the event, and we can use this to create a view of the world. But what happens if there is no general view of the world?

AI might make this possible. Google's 2013 Google Glass

looked like a pair of glasses, but with a camera and a small **projector**. The glasses were linked to a smartphone, which could cover whatever the user was seeing with a **projected** image. These types of applications are called augmented reality: they take the real world and cover it with computer-generated information or images.

But what about apps that do not augment reality, but completely change it in a way that users cannot see? We already have AI systems which create images that appear to be totally real to humans, but have actually been entirely created by a neural network. Deepfakes are pictures or videos which have been changed by a neural network to include people who were not present in the original. There are many well-known and worrying examples of this, including famous people in videos they did not participate in. At present, the quality of deepfake videos is poor, but it is getting better, and soon we will not be able to tell whether or not a photo or video is real. At that point, the idea of photos and videos providing a reliable record of events will no longer be true.

A further problem is Fake AI, where people are misled into believing that what they are seeing is AI when in fact there are human minds behind it. We have already looked at the possibility of this happening with programs such as ELIZA and Siri. It is unclear how many companies purposely fake their AI systems to suggest they have greater capabilities than they actually do. This is unhelpful to AI research as it prevents people trusting it.

CHAPTER SIXTEEN

Are conscious machines possible?

Strong AI, building machines that really have conscious minds, **self-awareness** and understanding, like us, is still a distant goal. We have no idea how or where to begin, or what we are dealing with; and there are no tests available to study or measure the mind or consciousness in any scientific way. You just cannot see what another person is thinking or experiencing, but we can identify some parts of consciousness. It must have the ability to experience things from a personal point of view. Philosophers call this qualia, the perceptions of the mind that we all experience, like the smell of coffee. The problem is that qualia are personal. So, although we think we are sharing the same experiences, there is no way of knowing if we are experiencing them in the same way as another person.

One of the most famous tests of consciousness was developed by the American philosopher Thomas Nagel in 1974. Nagel's test considers whether the question "What is it like to be an X?" is meaningful when applied to different things. If so, Nagel argued that the X had to be conscious. The question is meaningful when applied to humans, monkeys, dogs, and even rats; although there is no concrete evidence that they are conscious. What about simpler creatures like insects? It seems more doubtful that they are conscious, according to Nagel's test, although you could argue that they just have a far more basic consciousness than humans. Things like ovens or rocks clearly fail the consciousness test, as it does not feel like anything to be them.

The test brings attention to a number of important points. First, is consciousness an all-or-nothing thing, or does it have different levels? At one end there is human consciousness and at the other end the consciousness of insects. But even between humans, there are differences.

Second, is consciousness different for different things? Nagel's paper was called "What is it like to be a bat?", a title chosen because bats are so different to humans. Bats are conscious, according to Nagel's theory, but perceive things differently. They make very high sounds that humans cannot hear, and receive echoes that tell them about their environment. Since we cannot do this, we are unable to imagine what it is like to be a bat. Even though we think Nagel's question is meaningful, bat consciousness is so very different to human consciousness. It is impossible to understand what bat consciousness is, although we may be confident that it is there.

Nagel's test can be applied to computers, and most people seem to believe that it is not like anything to be a computer, any more than an oven. For this reason, Nagel's "What is it like" argument has been used to argue that strong AI is impossible, as computers cannot be conscious. Perhaps we cannot imagine what it would be like to be a computer just because they are so different to humans, but that does not necessarily mean that machine consciousness is impossible, just that it would be different.

There are many other arguments attempting to show strong AI to be impossible, such as the fact that people are special. But however amazing humans are, they are made of a group of atoms, the smallest chemical parts which everything in the universe is made of, so we are nothing special. But this does not answer the difficult question of how a particular group of atoms can lead to the conscious experience of humans.

Another argument is that much of human action and decision-making is based on the ability to understand something. This is done without the need for conscious reasoning, and it cannot be reduced to a program in the way that computers require. There is evidence that much of our decision-making is not based on explicit or careful reasoning. This probably comes from experience we have gained over time. And we have seen that computers can learn from experience and become effective decision-makers, too.

One of the most famous arguments against the possibility of strong AI is based on a scenario called the Chinese room. A man is working alone in a room and receives cards under the door on which questions are written in Chinese, a language he does not understand. He takes these cards, and then carefully follows written instructions to write an answer in Chinese, which he then passes back out of the room. In fact, the room is doing a Chinese Turing test, and the answers provided by the room convince the interviewers outside that it is human. There is no meaningful understanding present, as neither the man nor the room understand Chinese. The man's intelligence is used only to carefully follow the instructions he is given, just as a computer would. By the same argument, a computer passing the Turing test would not show understanding, so strong AI cannot be produced just by following a recipe, no matter how much your program appears to have understanding.

Another thing to consider is how a conscious mind helped humans to develop. One theory is that the conscious mind is actually nothing more than a meaningless by-product of the things in our body that actually produce our behaviour. Another view is that the conscious mind does not play a key part in our behaviour, but rather that it somehow comes from other processes in our brain. This mind-body problem is one of the biggest and oldest issues in science and philosophy and is not yet solved.

A key part of our conscious human experience is our ability to understand ourselves and others as part of a social group, and to be able to reason about others and about how others see us. This key capability most probably developed as a requirement for living and working together in large, complex social groups. British psychologist Robin Dunbar calculated that a human brain can manage on average 150 human relationships – which might tell us something about the number of people we actively interact with on social networking sites. So, we could conclude that the human brain is special because it is social.

Another central part of how humans look at and try to understand the world is by naturally identifying agents which are similar to them. Physical features like weight are used to predict a stone falling to the ground if dropped. However, this is not useful in understanding the behaviour of computers, and definitely not people. Design can be used to predict the behaviour of a system like a clock, using the numbers on its face to tell the time, which is what it is for. But the most useful way to predict and explain human behaviour is to suppose that a person's beliefs and desires will make them act **rationally**; a theory by philosopher Daniel Dennett known as the intentional stance, which can also be applied to machines.

Human use of the intentional stance is linked to the fact that we are social animals, required to understand and predict the behaviour of other agents in society. To return to Dunbar's research, which looked at the relationship between brain size and the capacity for higher-order intentional reasoning capabilities in humans and other animals, he found that brain size is strongly linked to social-group size. So it follows that a natural explanation for the development of large brains is the need for, and value of, social reasoning – higher-order intentional reasoning – within a complex society. This in turn could be linked to consciousness. But why might social reasoning require consciousness? And are there machines that are capable of social reasoning?

If a robot believes it is raining and it wants to stay dry, it should take appropriate action to prevent getting wet. If the robot did not take such action, then we would probably say either that it did not believe it was raining, or it did not really want to stay dry, or that it was not rational. The intentional stance is of greatest help when we do not understand the agent, as it explains and predicts behaviour independently of whether it is a person or a dog or a robot. If you are a rational agent with the desire to stay dry and the belief that it is raining, then I can explain and predict your behaviour without knowing anything else about you.

What does this tell us with respect to our dreams for AI? What could progress towards conscious machines look like, and how might we create it? Suppose we had a machine learning program that learns on its own, just as the DeepMind agent did in *Breakout*, to succeed in a scenario which requires meaningful, complex higher-order intentional reasoning? Or a scenario which requires an agent to tell a complex lie, using higher-order intentional reasoning? Or a scenario in which an agent learns to meaningfully share its state of mind and those of others? A system that could learn to do these things in a meaningful way would be some important way along the road to conscious machines.

An example of this is the Sally–Anne test. The test **consists** of a short story that is told or acted out to a child, who must answer questions based on the beliefs of other people. Theory of Mind (ToM) is the practical ability that fully developed adults have which allows them to reason about the beliefs and desires of others and themselves. Researchers recently developed a neural net system called ToMnet ("Theory of Mind net"), which is able to learn how to model other agents and behave correctly in Sally–Anne scenarios. The work is at a very early stage, and the ability to solve a Sally–Anne puzzle is not enough to say that a system has artificial consciousness, but it is a step in the right direction.

Suppose we succeeded in building machines with a human-level theory of mind; machines that autonomously learn to handle complex higher-order intentional reasoning, that can build and manage complex social relationships, that can express complex properties of their own mental state and those of others. Would those machines really have a "mind", consciousness, self-awareness? We just cannot answer this question at present. We should have a much better idea if we ever get closer to being able to build such machines.

———

At this point, I can feel the ghost of Alan Turing trying to get my attention. He argued that if a machine is doing something that is the same as the "real thing", then we should stop arguing about whether it is actually conscious or has self-perception. If we really cannot tell the difference, using any reasonable test that we can create, then that may be as much as we can ever ask.

During-reading questions

CHAPTER SEVEN

1 What were the two main research groups in AI in the early 1990s?
2 What was the name of the theory that Brooks developed and what did he design to show how it worked?

CHAPTER EIGHT

1 What was HOMER, where did it work and what did it do?
2 When did we first see an agent-based interface taking an active role and what form did that take?

CHAPTER NINE

1 What was the new challenge for multi-agent systems?
2 Which two important achievements helped AI become a recognized scientific field in the 1990s?

CHAPTER TEN

1 What is a machine learning program and what is a typical application of it?
2 Explain the problem of feature extraction in machine learning.

CHAPTER ELEVEN

1 What was *Breakout* and why was it important?
2 Which two areas of AI show the limitations of deep learning techniques and why?

CHAPTER TWELVE

1 Give examples of how AI is helping make changes in healthcare.
2 What are the main problems for driverless cars and what are the possible solutions?

CHAPTER THIRTEEN

1 What is the Singularity and why might it not be a serious problem?
2 Explain the Trolley Problem and how it can be applied to driverless cars.

CHAPTER FOURTEEN

1 Which jobs might be in danger, and which should be safe in the future, because of AI?
2 What are the ethical arguments for and against the use of autonomous drones in war?

CHAPTER FIFTEEN

1 Give some examples of bias in AI that have happened or could happen.
2 How does AI help spread fake news?

CHAPTER SIXTEEN

1 What is Nagel's test?
2 What is the Chinese room scenario and what does it say about strong AI?

After-reading questions

1 What have you learned about Artificial Intelligence that you didn't know before?

2 **a** What is the difference between strong AI and weak AI?
b Which do you think it is more important to develop?

3 What do you think has been the biggest achievement of AI so far and why?

4 What are the limitations of deep learning programs today?

5 In which areas of your life would you not want to rely on AI systems and why?

6 In twenty years' time, how do you think AI will have changed your life? Does this worry you or make you feel excited?

7 Should we be afraid of AI? Why/Why not?

Exercises

1 Write the correct names in your notebook.

> David Hilbert   An American team   Konrad Zuse
> John von Neumann   Alan Turing
> Joseph Weizenbaum

1 _David Hilbert_   first asked if there are decision problems that cannot be answered by simply following mathematical steps

2 ....   invented a mathematical problem-solving machine for decision problems

3 ....   designed a computer called the Z3 in Germany during the Second World War

4 ....   developed a machine called ENIAC to calculate information required for firing guns over long distances

5 ....   gave his name to the basic design for the modern computer

6 ....   wrote a famous computer program called ELIZA, which asked questions to patients about their feelings

2 Put these problems in order of how hard they are to write code for, with 1 as the easiest and 6 as the hardest.

a .... understanding a painting

b .... playing board games

c ....1.... mathematical calculations

d .... driverless cars

e .... automated translation

f .... arranging lists of numbers

3 Put these words into four groups in your notebook.

| *Call of Duty* | PowerPoint | Java | SHAKEY |
| *Minecraft* | Word | Python | STRIPS |

AI systems	Computer games	Computer programs	Computer programming languages
	Call of Duty		

4 **Choose the correct form of the verb to complete these sentences in your notebook.**

1 If we can build programs to solve problems that people find hard, then surely this **will / would** be an important step on the road to AI.

2 If there is a solution, we **will find / would have found** it in the end using this process.

3 If you **do / did** a quick experiment, you would see that in almost all possible combinations of the puzzle there would be three ways to move.

4 Now suppose you **have / had** 100 people, and you need a team of fifty. Then you would have to check 100 billion billion billion possible teams.

5 This means that if you could find a quick recipe, or program, for solving just one NP-complete problem, then you **will find / would have found** a recipe for solving all of them.

6 It simply depends on whether you **can accept / could have accepted** the pattern of reasoning, and the conclusions you come to, if the premises were true.

CHAPTER SEVEN

5 Match the words together. Then write sentences in your notebook about the six required behaviours of the vacuum cleaning robot.

Example: 1 – b It avoids obstacles if it perceives them.

1	avoid	**a**	a direction
2	shut	**b**	obstacles
3	empty	**c**	dock
4	return to	**d**	down
5	switch	**e**	dirt
6	choose	**f**	on

CHAPTER EIGHT

6 Complete this conversation between a human and HOMER with the correct words in your notebook.

> Yes.   No.   8.56 p.m.
> I'll go to the port in order to pick up the parcel.   On the boat.

1 Human: Are you going to the port next Saturday?
HOMER: ....*Yes.*............

2 Human: Why are you going to the port?
HOMER: ....

3 Human: What time are you going to pick it up?
HOMER: ....

4 Human: Where will the parcel be next Sunday?
HOMER: ....

5 Human: Will the parcel be at the port a week from now?
HOMER: ....

7 **Match the two parts of these sentences in your notebook.**
Example: 1 – f

1 In this case, if your agent were given a choice between an apple and an orange, and chose an orange,

2 So, for the first example,

3 However, if you only include a small number of features in your training data,

4 For example, reinforcement learning

5 Of course, the neural nets that we see in nature contain many neurons, connecting in many different ways,

6 While PDP and backprop made a lot of new applications possible for neural nets,

a by the mid-1990s progress had once again slowed.

b is widely used to train programs.

c so more complex perceptron models were developed.

d we could say that the utility of an orange is 3, the utility of a pear is 2 and the utility of an apple is 1.

e you may accidentally leave out features needed to allow the program to learn correctly.

f you would be happy.

8 Are these sentences *true* or *false*? Write the correct answers in your notebook.

1 In an image-captioning problem, you want a computer to take an image and describe it through text. ....*true*..........

2 Translation programs can now successfully translate the complex language of novels.

3 In April 2019, scientists used AI to take the first ever pictures of a black hole.

4 AlphaFold is a system to help treat serious medical conditions like Alzheimer's disease, using machine learning techniques to predict future signs of the disease.

5 Neural nets cannot yet automatically identify eye problems above or at the level of human experts.

6 Probably the best driverless car technology you can buy today is Tesla's Autopilot, which has high automation.

CHAPTER THIRTEEN

9 **Complete these sentences with the correct information in your notebook.**

> The Three Laws of Robotics   A general rule of good actions
> Virtue ethics   The greatest happiness principle
> Consequentialist reasoning   The Asilomar principles

1 _The Three Laws of Robotics_ were created in a series of stories about robots with a kind of strong AI.

2 .... decides on the ethics of actions based on their results.

3 .... says that one should act for the greatest good for society.

4 .... means not taking any action, because taking any life is wrong, even though not acting leads to five other deaths.

5 .... identifies a decision-maker with good ethics and tries to act like they would in the situation.

6 .... was one of the first and most important systems of ethical AI, which had twenty-three rules.

10 **Make compound nouns for these sentences in your notebook.**

1 As a general-......*purpose*.......... technology, AI can be misused or have unintended consequences.

2 Since 2001, remote-.......... drones, flown from a distance, have been used by the USA in wars in countries like Afghanistan, Pakistan and Yemen.

3 As machine learning systems have been applied to more areas, we have begun to understand how automated decision-.......... systems can show algorithmic bias.

4 Sometimes, the bias is explicit, such as in the TIMIT spoken-.......... data widely used to train speech understanding programs.

5 These types of applications are called augmented reality: they take the real world and cover it with computer-.......... information or images.

6 Strong AI, building machines that really have conscious minds, self-.......... and understanding, like us, is still a distant goal.

Project work

1 Write a review of a system you could use in your daily life which uses AI technology (virtual assistant, image captioning, automated translation, augmented reality glasses, etc.). Include information about:
- what it is and how it works,
- what's good and bad about it,
- whether or not you would tell other people to buy/ use it and why.

2 Write a newspaper article predicting how we will be living in fifty years' time in an environment where AI is widely used. In your article consider the following areas of life:
- education and work
- travel and free time
- health and well-being
- crime and safety.

3 Have a debate about one of the following questions:
- Should machines be designed to be ethical?
- What can we do about fake news, deepfakes pictures or videos?
- Are conscious machines possible and do we even want them?
- Will robots make us unemployed one day soon?
- What decisions would you not be happy for a machine to make?

Essay questions

1 What is so special about being human and can a machine
ever really copy that? (500 words)

2 According to the author of this book, what will AI systems
soon be capable of doing and how will that change people's
lives in the near future? (500 words)

3 A university or college is considering using a machine
learning program to correct students' essays. It will be able
to quickly check that students are not cheating or copying
from the internet and it will decide on the grade to be
given to each student. Discuss the possible effects of this
technology. (500 words)

An answer key for all questions and exercises can be found at
www.penguinreaders.co.uk

Glossary

algorithm (n.)
a set of rules that a computer uses for solving problems or calculating things

application (n.); **app** (n.)
An *application* of something is the way that it can be used for a particular purpose. An *app* is a computer program, especially on a mobile phone, that helps you to do a particular thing. *App* is short for *application*.

artificial intelligence (**AI**) (n.)
using computer technology to make computers and other machines think and do things in the way that people can

automated (adj.); **automation** (n.)
If something is *automated*, it uses or is done by machines and not by people. *Automation* is the noun of *automated*.

automatically (adv.)
1) done by machine, without people having to do anything
2) without thinking about something

autonomous (adj.)
able to do things and make decisions without help

base (v.)
If something is *based* on an idea, fact, etc., it has been developed by using that idea, fact, etc. in an important way.

behaviour (n.)
what a person or thing does, or how a person or thing does something. *Behaviour* is the noun of *behave*.

bias (n.); **biased** (adj.)
Bias is when you treat a person or thing in a way that is unfair or different from the way that you treat others. If someone or something does this, they are *biased* towards or against that person or thing.

capability (n.)
the ability to do something

checkers (n.)
a game for two people which is played by moving flat, round pieces across a board with black and white squares

chess (n.)
a game for two people which is played by moving pieces with different shapes and names (King, castle, etc.) around a board with black and white squares

circuit (n.)
a path that is shaped like a circle.
An electrical *circuit* is the path that
electricity travels around.

classification (n.); **classify** (v.)
To *classify* things is to put them into
groups according to their type, size,
etc. *Classification* is the noun of
classify.

complex (adj.)
A *complex* thing has a lot of
different parts and is difficult to
understand.

computer processor (n.)
the main part of a computer which
controls the other parts of the
system

conclude (v); **conclusion** (n.)
If you *conclude* something, or if you
come to or reach a *conclusion*, you
decide what is true after thinking
about or studying something
carefully.

conscious (adj);
consciousness (n.)
able to think and know or
understand what is happening.
Consciousness is the noun of *conscious*.

consequent (adj);
consequence (n.)
In an 'IF . . . THEN . . .' rule,
as used in an *expert system*, the
consequent is the *conclusion* – the part
immediately after the 'THEN'.

consist (v.)
If something *consists of* two or more
things, it is made of those things.

consistent (adj.);
consistently (adv.)
If something is *consistent*, it happens
in the same way and does not
change. *Consistently* is the adverb of
consistent.

corresponding (adj.)
matching or connected with
something

data (n.)
information or facts used for
calculating things or making
decisions

deduction (n.); **deduce** (v.)
getting new knowledge from
knowledge you already have.

device (n.)
a machine or tool that you use
for doing particular things, like a
mobile phone, laptop, etc.

dexterity (n.); **dexterous** (adj.)
Dexterity is skill in using your hands or mind. A *dexterous* person has this skill.

diagnose (v.) **diagnosis** (n.)
A doctor *diagnoses* an illness when they decide what is wrong with someone after asking them questions and examining their body. This decision is the doctor's *diagnosis*. We say *diagnoses* for two or more of them. A computer *system* can also *diagnose* a problem and make a *diagnosis*.

digital (adj.)
1) sending and receiving information like pictures, sounds, etc. by changing it into a series of numbers or electronic signals
2) connected with computer technology or the internet

docking station (n.)
You connect a laptop, phone or other *mobile device* to a *docking station* in order to get electricity for it or to connect it with other *devices*.

efficient (adj.); **efficiently** (adv.)
working well and in the best way. *Efficiently* is the adverb of *efficient*.

ethics (n.); **ethical** (adj.)
Ethics is ideas and beliefs about what is right or wrong. *Ethical* is the adjective of *ethics*.

explicit (adj.); **explicitly** (adv.)
If something is *explicit* or is done *explicitly*, it is said or done in an extremely clear way and so is easy to see or understand.

fake (adj.)
not real

hardware (n.)
the machines and electronic parts in a computer. Computer programs are *software*.

homosexuality (n.)
when you are sexually attracted to people who are the same sex as you

inconsistent (adj.)
If something is *inconsistent*, it does not always happen in the same way or stay the same.

ingredient (n.)
one of the parts or qualities of something that are needed to make it successful. The key *ingredients* are the most important.

input (n.)
information that a computer,
computer program, etc. receives

interact (v.); **interaction** (n.)
when two or more people or things
communicate with each other,
or have an effect on each other.
Interaction is the noun of *interact*.

interface (n.)
the part of a computer *system* that
passes information between one
part of the *system* and another, or
between the computer *system* and
the *user*

intervene (v.);
intervention (n.)
when a person or thing becomes
involved in a situation in order to
help or improve it, or to stop a bad
thing from happening. *Intervention* is
the noun of *intervene*.

law (n.)
a rule in science, mathematics, etc.
which explains something that is
always true

level (n.)
1) a person or thing's ability
compared to other people or things
2) a height or position within
something
3) an amount of something

limitation (n.)
The *limitations* of something are
the things it is not good at doing or
cannot do.

logic (n.); **logical** (adj.);
logically (adv.)
Logic is the way that a person or
thing connects ideas when they
are explaining something or giving
reasons. It is also the name for the
science that studies and describes
this. If something is *logical*, it
connects ideas or reasons in a
sensible way. *Logically* is the adverb
of *logical*.

map (v.); **mapping** (n.)
If you *map* one of a certain group
of things to a particular thing
in a different group, you make
a connection between the two
things. The connection is called a
mapping. To *map* a place or thing
also means to make a map of it or
give information about how it is
organized.

mobile (adj.)
1) able to move around
2) easy to move and use in different
places

model (v.); **model** (n.)
To *model* something is to create a description or copy of it so that you can study it carefully. The description or copy that you create is a *model*.

navigate (v.)
to find a way around or to a place

network (n.)
a group of similar things, computers or *devices* for example, that are connected together and can share information

obstacle (n.)
1) an object that you must go around before you can continue to move
2) a problem that makes it more difficult to do something or prevents you from doing it

output (n.)
information that a computer, computer program, etc. produces

perception (n.); **perceive** (v.)
understanding what is around you in your environment

power (n.); **powerful** (adj.)
Power is energy, like electricity, that makes machines work. *Power* is also the ability to work well and do things. A *powerful* thing works very well and can do a lot.

precise (adj.); **precisely** (adv.)
accurate and exact. *Precisely* is the adverb of *precise*. *Imprecise* is the opposite of *precise*.

predict (v.); **prediction** (n.)
If you *predict* something or make a *prediction*, you say or write what you think will happen in the future.

process (n. and v.)
A *process* is a series of stages or steps that lead to a certain result. If a computer *processes data*, it receives the *data* and does things with it so that it can use and understand it.

projector (n.);
projected (adj.)
A *projector* is a machine that puts images, films, etc. on to a screen or wall. A *projected* image has been sent to a screen by a *projector*.

puzzle (n.)
a game or activity in which you have to think carefully and put pieces together correctly, or answer questions

random (adj.); **randomly** (adv.)
If something is done *at random* or *randomly*, it is done without thinking or making a decision about it before it happens.

rational (adj.);
rationally (adv.)
based on facts and sensible reasons rather than what people feel or imagine. *Rationally* is the adverb of *rational*.

reasoning (n.); **reason** (v.)
Reasoning is when you think about something carefully in order to make a decision. To *reason* is to have the ability to think and understand and make sensible decisions. If you *reason* that something is true, you decide that it is true after considering the facts.

recipe (n.)
A *recipe* is a set of instructions that tells you how to cook something and gives a list of the food you need. In this text, a *recipe* is a set of instructions used in mathematics or for a computer, etc.

represent (v.)
1) to be a sign or *symbol* for something
2) to be an example of something
3) to speak for or show the opinions of a group of people

representative (adj.)
typical of a particular group of things or people

responsibility (n.)
a duty (= something that you should or must do) to deal with or take care of something

risk (n. and v.); **risky** (adj.)
A *risk* is a chance that something bad might happen. To *risk* doing something is to do it even when something bad might happen because of it. If something is *risky*, it involves a lot of *risks*.

robotics (n.)
the science of designing, building and using robots

satellite navigation system (n.)
a computer *system*, often used in cars, that uses information from satellites (= things that are sent into space to send pictures and information to Earth) to tell you where you are or the best way to get to a place

scenario (n.)
a description of possible actions or events

self-aware (adj.);
self-awareness (n.)
knowing and understanding your
own abilities, thoughts, etc. *Self-
awareness* is the noun of *self-aware*.

sense (v.); **sensor** (n.)
understanding the environment
you are in. *Sensors* on machines are
usually things like cameras.

sequence (n.)
a set of things, actions or events
which have a particular order

simulated (adj.);
simulation (n.)
If something is *simulated* or is a
simulation, it is made to look
or behave like a real thing or
situation, but it is not real.

stimulate (v.)
to make something develop or
become more active

symbol (n.)
a mark, picture or letter that is
used to *represent* something. "+" is
a *symbol*.

system (n.)
1) a group of things, like
computers, computer programs,
etc., that are connected and work
together to do a particular thing
2) a way of organizing or doing
things

systematically (adv.)
If something is done *systematically*,
it is done in a careful and
complete way and follows a *system*.

task (n.)
something that you have to do

technique (n.)
a special way of doing something

theory (n.); **theoretical** (adj.)
A *theory* is an idea that tries to
explain why something happens.
If something is *theoretical*, it
is *based on* ideas and not real
experience or use.

transform (v.)
You change something
completely so that it becomes
another thing. You *transform* one
thing into another.

translate (v.)
1) to change information from one form to another
2) to change speech or writing from one language to another
3) to lead to a particular result

translation (n.)
the activity of changing speech or writing from one language to another

transparency (n.)
the quality of being clear and easy to understand

typical (adj.)
having qualities that are like most things or people from a particular group. A *typical* person or thing shows what a particular kind of person or thing is usually like.

update (v.)
to add the most recent information to something

user (n.)
a person or thing that uses something, for example a computer *system*

vacuum cleaner (n.);
vacuum (v.)
A *vacuum cleaner* is a machine that picks up dirt from the floor or carpet. To *vacuum* is to clean something using a *vacuum cleaner*.

virtual reality (n.)
images and sounds that are produced by a computer but seem real to a *user* because they can *interact* with them

World Wide Web (n.)
a very large collection of documents, websites, pictures, sounds, etc. which are connected on the internet

Technical glossary

activation threshold
the point at which an artificial *neuron* is *stimulated* to produce an *output*.

adversarial machine learning
when you try to trick a machine learning program by giving it *inputs* that are maybe obvious to humans, but which lead to an incorrect *output*

agent
a complete *AI system*, which has lots of different *AI capabilities* so that it can work for a *user* independently

algorithmic bias
the possibility that *AI systems* will show *bias* when making decisions, because they are *trained* with *biased data* groups or because of badly designed *software*

backpropagation
the most important *algorithm* for *training neural nets*

behavioural AI
a type of *AI* with its attention on *behaviours*, or the different things a *system* should do, before considering how the *systems* are linked

Blocks World
a small *simulated* world in which an *AI system* has to arrange things like boxes

branching factor
the number of choices you have to consider every time you make a decision. When playing a game, it is the number of ways you can move on average from a particular board position.

combinatorial explosion
a basic problem in AI when you use *search*, because each choice in a *sequence* quickly increases the number of possibilities you need to consider

decidable problem
a problem that can be solved by an *algorithm*. An *undecidable problem* cannot be solved in this way.

decision problem
a mathematical problem that has a yes/no answer.

deep learning
important machine learning *techniques* that use deeper, *neural nets* with more connections; bigger, carefully chosen *training data* groups; and some new *techniques*

depth-first search
a type of *search technique* used in *problem solving*, which expands just one branch of a *search tree* instead of the whole tree *layer* by *layer*

emergent property
when a *system* shows something unexpected because of the way that different parts of the *system* affect each other

expert system
a *system* that uses human expert knowledge to solve problems in one particular and limited area

feature
the parts of a piece of *data* or *data group* that a machine learning program uses to make its decisions

feature extraction
the problem of deciding which *features* in a *data* group should be selected to *train* a program in machine learning

first-order logic
a very general language, developed to give a *precise* starting point for mathematical *reasoning*

General AI
the goal of building *AI systems* with all the abilities that humans have

goal state
how we want our problem to look when we have successfully completed a problem-solving *task*

heuristic search, heuristics
a way of using *search* to try to find a solution, without knowing if you are moving in the right direction

high-level programming language
a programming language like Python or Java, which works on different types of computers and hides the low-level details of the computer it is running on

initial state
what a problem looks like before we have completed a problem-solving *task*

knowledge base
in an expert *system*, human expert knowledge, often coded in the form of rules.

knowledge-based AI
using human *expert* knowledge about problems to write the code for programs, often in the form of rules

knowledge representation
the problem of how to write knowledge as a code that computers can use

logic-based AI
a type of *AI* in which intelligent
decision-making is reduced to
logical reasoning, as with *first-order
logic*

machine learning
one of the basic *capabilities* of
an intelligent *system*. A machine
learning program learns to link
inputs and *outputs* without being
told how.

multi-agent systems
systems in which lots of agents
interact with each other

neural nets
machine learning using "artificial
neurons", the basic *technique* used in
deep learning

neuron
a type of cell, the smallest part
of a living thing, that receives
and sends messages to, from, and
between different parts of the
brain

NP-complete problem
a type of computer problem that is
hard to solve *efficiently*

perceptron model
a type of *neural net*, studied
in the 1960s, which is still
important today

planning
the problem of finding a *sequence*
of actions that will change an
initial state into a *goal state*

**preference, preference
relation**
how you grade every pair of
possible choices according to which
one you prefer, so that an agent
working for you can make the best
possible choice of what you want

problem solving
finding the right *sequence* of actions
to move from the *initial state* to the
goal state of a problem

reinforcement learning
a type of machine learning,
in which an agent acts in its
environment and receives reports
on its actions in the form of
rewards

representation harm
one of two types of harm that
can be caused by *biased* computer
programs. When a *system* acts to
create or support a widely held,
general image or opinion of
someone or something that is not
based on fact. The other type of
harm is allocative harm, when a
particular group is or is not chosen
unfairly based on some *feature*, or
piece of *data*.

reward
the positive or negative report
that a *reinforcement learning* program
receives on its actions

search, search tree
a basic *AI* problem-solving *technique*,
in which a computer program tries
to find how to achieve a goal by
starting from some *initial state*, using
a limited range of actions and then
creating a *search tree*

Singularity
a point at which we imagine
machine intelligence could pass
human intelligence

software agent
an agent that is part of a computer
environment but not the physical
world. Software robots are
examples of software agents.

strong AI
the goal of building *AI systems* that
really do have mind, *consciousness*,
awareness and so on in the way
that we do

subsumption architecture
a way of organizing the *behaviours*
of a robot so that more desired
behaviours come before less desired
behaviours. For a *vacuuming* robot, this
could mean that avoiding *obstacles* is
more important than cleaning.

supervised learning
the simplest type of machine
learning, where we *train* a program
by showing it examples of *inputs*
and desired *outputs*

symbolic AI
a type of *AI* that involves *modelling*
reasoning and planning *processes*

TouringMachines
a type of agent designed with
controls divided into three *layers*
responsible for: reacting, planning
and *modelling*

training
giving a machine learning program
examples of *inputs* and *outputs* so
that it can learn the links between
them without being told

uncertainty
A typical problem in *AI*, *uncertainty*
occurs with situations in which
the information provided was not
known to be definitely true.

undecidable problem
a mathematical problem that
we know cannot be solved by a
computer or a Turing machine

universal basic income
the idea that everyone in society
should receive a certain amount of
money, whether or not they work

utility, expected utility
numbers used to represent
preferences in *AI* programs. The
expected utility is the average *utility*
that you could expect to get from
the choice of a particular course
of action.

weak AI
the goal of building machines
which appear to have
understanding (*consciousness*,
mind, self-perception, and so on)
without *explicitly* saying that they
actually have these things

Acknowledgements

[1] adapted from A. Hodges, *Alan Turing: The Enigma*, Burnett Books Ltd. 1983

[2] adapted from A. M. Turing, "Computing Machinery and Intelligence", *Mind*, 49, 1950, pp. 433–60

[3] adapted from P. Winston and B. Horn, *LISP* (3rd edn) Pearson, 1989

[4] adapted from J. McCarthy, *Concepts of Logical AI*, Unpublished note

[5] D. E. Rumelhart and J. L. McClelland (eds) *Parallel Distributed Processing* (2 vols.) MIT Press, 1986

[6] adapted from V. Dignum, *Responsible Artificial Intelligence*, Springer, 2019

[7] adapted from C. B. Benedikt Frey and M. A. Osborne, "The Future of Employment: How Susceptible Are Jobs to Computerisation?" *Technological Forecasting and Social Change*, 114, January 2017

[8] adapted from R. Arkin, "Governing Lethal Behaviour: Embedding Ethics in a Hybrid Deliberative/Reactive Robot Architecture", Technical report GIT-GVU-07-11, College of Computing, Georgia Institute of Technology

[9] adapted from C. Criado Perez, *Invisible Women: Exposing Data Bias in a World Designed for Men*, Chatto & Windus, 2019

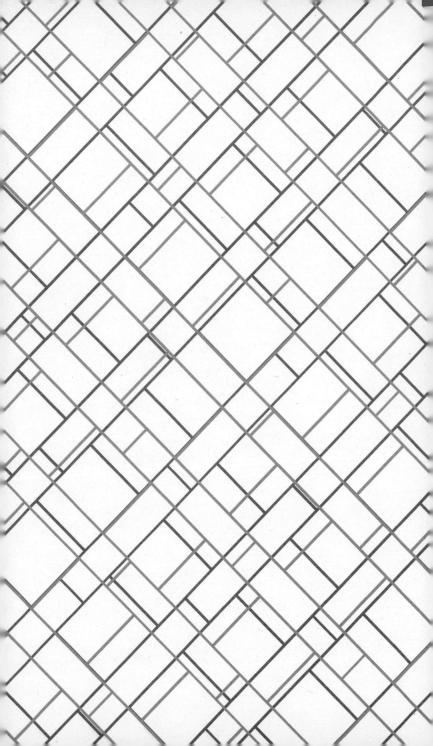

Penguin (🐧) Readers

Visit **www.penguinreaders.co.uk**
for FREE Penguin Readers resources
and digital and audio versions of this book.